**SUMMER BEFORE 3**

SO-CFK-562

# SUMMER LINK
# BASIC LEARNING SKILLS

McGraw-Hill Children's Publishing

Columbus, Ohio

 **Children's Publishing**

Copyright © 2004 McGraw-Hill Children's Publishing. Published by
American Education Publishing, an imprint of McGraw-Hill Children's Publishing,
a Division of The McGraw-Hill Companies.

Send all inquiries to:
McGraw-Hill Children's Publishing
8787 Orion Place
Columbus, OH 43240-4027

ISBN 0-7696-3562-8

1 2 3 4 5 6 7 8 9 10 VHJ 09 08 07 06 05 04

*The McGraw·Hill Companies*

# Table of Contents

# Summer Link Recommended Reading

- **Animal Close-Ups Series** by Barbara Taylor
- **Araminta's Paint Box; Song and Dance Man** by Karen Ackerman
- **The Arctic; The Desert; The Ocean; The Rain Forest** by Alan Baker
- **Barn Dance!** by Bill Martin, Jr.
- **Bird Watch: A Book of Poetry** by Jane Yolen
- **Chester's Way; Julius, the Baby of the World** by Kevin Henkes
- **Chickens Aren't the Only Ones** by Ruth Heller
- **Dandelions; Fly Away Home** by Eve Bunting
- **Fox In Love** (first reader) by Edward Marshall
- **Good Driving, Amelia Bedelia** by Herman Parish
- **The Great Kapok Tree** by Lynne Cherry
- **Henry and Mudge Series** (first readers) by Cynthia Rylant
- **Ira Says Goodbye** by Bernard Waber
- **Little Critter Series** (first readers) by Mercer Mayer
- **Miss Rumphius** by Barbara Cooney
- **Molly and Emmett's Camping Adventure; Molly and Emmett's Surprise Garden** by Marylin Hafner
- **The Napping House** by Audrey and Don Wood
- **Noisy Nora** by Rosemary Wells
- **The Ox-Cart Man** by Donald Hall
- **Why Mosquitoes Buzz In People's Ears** by Verna Aardema
- **Wolves** by R.D. Lawrence

# Number Knowledge: 2's, 5's, 10's

**Directions:** Write the missing numbers.

Count by 2's:

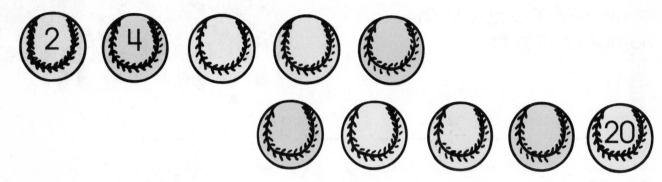

Count by 5's:

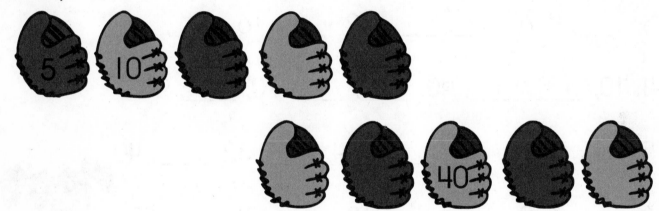

Count by 10's:

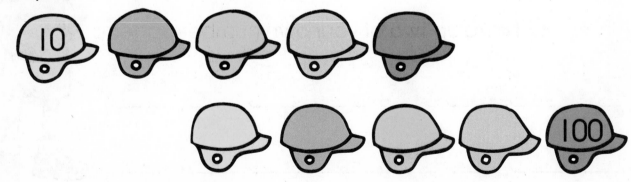

# Number Knowledge: Finding Patterns

Mia likes to count by twos, threes, fours, fives, tens, and hundreds.

**Directions:** Complete the number patterns.

1. 5, _____, _____, 20, _____, _____, 35, _____, _____, 50

2. 100, _____, _____, 400, _____, _____, _____, 800, _____

3. _____, 4, 6, _____, _____, 12, _____, 16, _____, _____

4. 10, _____, _____, 40, _____, _____, 70, _____, 90

5. 4, _____, 12, _____, _____, 24, _____, 32, _____, 40

6. _____, 6, 9, _____, _____, 18, _____, 24, _____, 30

**Directions:** Make up two of your own number patterns.

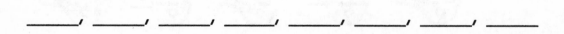

_____, _____, _____, _____, _____, _____, _____, _____

_____, _____, _____, _____, _____, _____, _____, _____

# Place Value: Hundreds, Tens, and Ones

**Directions:** Count the groups of crayons. Write the number of hundreds, tens, and ones.

**Example:**

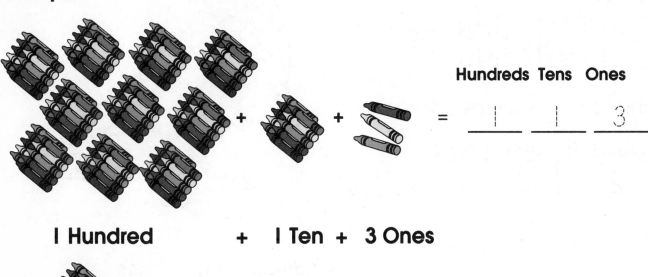

|         | Hundreds | Tens | Ones |
|---------|----------|------|------|
| =       | 1        | 1    | 3    |

I Hundred    +    I Ten  +  3 Ones

= _____ _____ _____

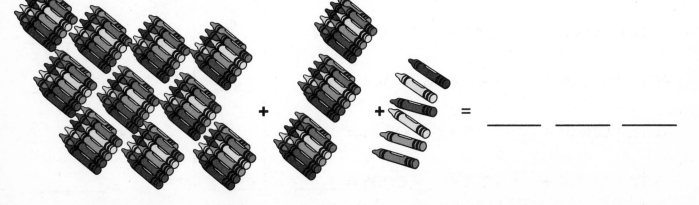

= _____ _____ _____

# Place Value: Count 'Em Up!

**Directions:** Look at the examples. Then, write the missing numbers in the blanks.

**Example:**

2 hundreds + 3 tens + 6 ones =

| hundreds | tens | ones |
|----------|------|------|
| 2 | 3 | 6 | = <u>236</u>

| | hundreds | tens | ones | |
|---|----------|------|------|---|
| 3 hundreds + 4 tens + 8 ones = | 3 | 4 | 8 | = _____ |
| ___ hundreds + ___ ten + ___ ones = | 2 | 1 | 7 | = _____ |
| ___ hundreds + ___ tens + ___ ones = | 6 | 3 | 5 | = _____ |
| ___ hundreds + ___ tens + ___ ones = | 4 | 7 | 9 | = _____ |
| ___ hundreds + ___ tens + ___ ones = | 2 | 9 | 4 | = _____ |
| ___ hundreds + ___ tens + ___ ones = | 4 | <u>2</u> | <u>0</u> | = _____ |
| 3 hundreds + 1 ten + 3 ones = ____ | ____ | ____ | = _____ |
| 3 hundreds + ___ tens + 7 ones = ____ | | 5 | | = _____ |
| 6 hundreds + 2 tens + ___ ones = ____ | ____ | | 8 | = _____ |

# Addition: Busy Bees

**Directions:** Look at the examples. Follow the steps to add.

**Examples:**
$$33 \\ +41$$
$$42 \\ +24$$

**Step 1:** Add the ones.

| tens | ones |
|------|------|
| 3 | 3 |
| +4 | 1 |
| | 4 |

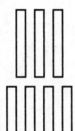 

**Step 2:** Add the tens.

| tens | ones |
|------|------|
| 3 | 3 |
| +4 | 1 |
| 7 | 4 |

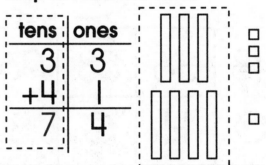

**Step 1:** Add the ones.

| tens | ones |
|------|------|
| 4 | 2 |
| +2 | 4 |
| | 6 |

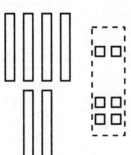

**Step 2:** Add the tens.

| tens | ones |
|------|------|
| 4 | 2 |
| +2 | 4 |
| 6 | 6 |

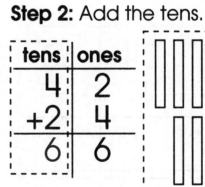 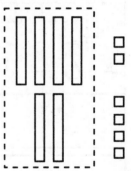

$$33 \\ +41$$
$$15 \\ +23$$
$$38 \\ +61$$
$$11 \\ +26$$
$$37 \\ +42$$
$$72 \\ +11$$

$$25 \\ +42$$
$$62 \\ +14$$
$$32 \\ +44$$
$$25 \\ +13$$
$$82 \\ + 6$$
$$91 \\ + 5$$

Name _____

# Addition: Anchors Away

**Directions:** Solve the addition problems. Use the code to find the answer to this riddle:

What did the pirate have to do before every trip out to sea?

| 48 | 36 | 58 | 96 | 69 | 75 | 89 | 29 |
|----|----|----|----|----|----|----|----|
| O | H | G | B | T | E | N | A |

| 42<br>+16 | 34<br>+41 | 60<br>+ 9 |
|-----------|-----------|-----------|
| 58 | | |

| | | |
|---|---|---|
| G | | |

| 17<br>+31 | 55<br>+34 |
|-----------|-----------|
| | |

| | |
|---|---|

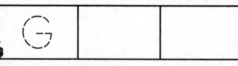

| 26<br>+43 | 14<br>+22 | 52<br>+23 |
|-----------|-----------|-----------|
| | | |

| | | |
|---|---|---|

| 83<br>+13 | 24<br>+24 | 5<br>+24 | 52<br>+17 |
|-----------|-----------|----------|-----------|
| | | | |

| | | | ! |
|---|---|---|---|

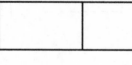

# Addition: Something's Fishy

**Directions:** Add the ones. Regroup if needed. Add the tens.

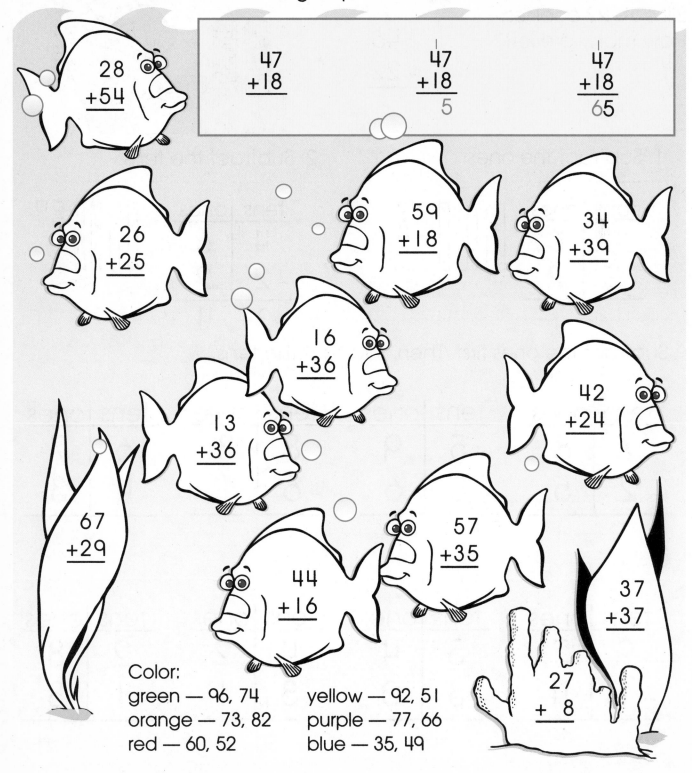

47
+18

47
+18
5

47
+18
65

28
+54

26
+25

59
+18

34
+39

16
+36

13
+36

42
+24

67
+29

44
+16

57
+35

37
+37

27
+ 8

Color:
green — 96, 74      yellow — 92, 51
orange — 73, 82     purple — 77, 66
red — 60, 52        blue — 35, 49

# Subtraction: Cookie Mania

**Directions:** There are 46 cookies.
Bill eats 22 cookies.
How many are left?

```
  46
- 22
-----
```

1. Subtract the ones.

| tens | ones |
|------|------|
| 4 | 6 |
| - 2 | 2 |

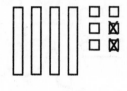

2. Subtract the tens.

| tens | ones |
|------|------|
| 4 | 6 |
| - 2 | 2 |
| 2 | 4 |

Subtract the ones first. Then, subtract the tens.

| tens | ones |
|------|------|
| 7 | 8 |
| - 2 | 5 |

| tens | ones |
|------|------|
| 5 | 9 |
| - 3 | 6 |

| tens | ones |
|------|------|
| 8 | 3 |
| - 6 | 1 |

| tens | ones |
|------|------|
| 6 | 7 |
| - 4 | 3 |

| tens | ones |
|------|------|
| 9 | 7 |
| - 1 | 4 |

| tens | ones |
|------|------|
| 5 | 4 |
| - 3 | 0 |

| tens | ones |
|------|------|
| 4 | 2 |
| - 3 | 1 |

| tens | ones |
|------|------|
| 2 | 8 |
| - 1 | 8 |

Name _____

# Subtraction: Mountaintop Getaway

**Directions:** Solve the problems. Find a path to the cabin by shading in all answers that have a 3 in them.

| | | | 98<br>−52 | 46<br>−12 | 68<br>−17 |
|---|---|---|---|---|---|
| | | 79<br>−53 | 65<br>−23 | 63<br>−31 | 86<br>−32 |
| | 59<br>−45 | 75<br>−64 | 67<br>−24 | 87<br>−54 | 55<br>−43 |
| 87<br>−65 | 44<br>−32 | 57<br>−24 | 88<br>−25 | 75<br>−61 | 48<br>−26 |
| 69<br>−25 | 95<br>−24 | 48<br>−13 | 58<br>−16 | 35<br>−13 | 39<br>−17 |

SECRET PATHS

# Subtraction: Undersea Adventure

## Steps for Subtracting

1. Do you regroup?

2. Subtract the ones.

3. Subtract the tens.

|  | tens | ones |  |  | tens | ones |  |
|---|---|---|---|---|---|---|---|
|  | 3 | 12 |  |  | 3 | 7 |  |
|  | 4̶ | 2̶ | Regroup? | − | 1 | 4 | Regroup? |
| − | 2 | 4 | Yes. | | 2 | 3 | No. |
|  | 1 | 8 |  |  |  |  |  |

**Directions:** Solve the subtraction problems below.

| tens | ones | | tens | ones | | tens | ones |
|---|---|---|---|---|---|---|---|
| 4 | 7 | | 6 | 4 | | 5 | 3 |
| -2 | 8 | | -3 | 4 | | -3 | 9 |

```
  56        83           43           75
- 27      - 47         - 39         - 53


  73        35           67           26
- 66      - 14         - 58         -  7
```

Name _____

# Addition and Subtraction: Go "Fore" It!

**Directions:** Add or subtract using regrouping.

| tens | ones |
|------|------|
| 2 | 15 |
| ~~3~~ | ~~5~~ |
| -2 | 7 |
| | 8 |

$$\begin{array}{r} 56 \\ -\ 27 \\ \hline \end{array}$$

$$\begin{array}{r} 40 \\ -\ 16 \\ \hline \end{array}$$

$$\begin{array}{r} 44 \\ +28 \\ \hline \end{array}$$

$$\begin{array}{r} 93 \\ -\ 39 \\ \hline \end{array}$$

$$\begin{array}{r} 42 \\ -14 \\ \hline \end{array}$$

$$\begin{array}{r} 97 \\ -\ 48 \\ \hline \end{array}$$

$$\begin{array}{r} 73 \\ -\ 24 \\ \hline \end{array}$$

$$\begin{array}{r} 33 \\ +18 \\ \hline \end{array}$$

$$\begin{array}{r} 56 \\ -\ 17 \\ \hline \end{array}$$

$$\begin{array}{r} 68 \\ -\ 49 \\ \hline \end{array}$$

$$\begin{array}{r} 49 \\ +32 \\ \hline \end{array}$$

$$\begin{array}{r} 77 \\ -\ 68 \\ \hline \end{array}$$

$$\begin{array}{r} 27 \\ +19 \\ \hline \end{array}$$

# Place Value: Hundreds

The place value of a digit or numeral is shown by where it is in the number. For example, in the number 123, 1 has the place value of hundreds, 2 is tens, and 3 is ones.

**Directions:** Study the examples. Then write the missing numbers in the blanks.

**Examples:**

2 hundreds + 3 tens + 6 ones =          1 hundreds + 4 tens + 9 ones =

| hundreds | tens | ones | |
|----------|------|------|--------|
| 2 | 3 | 6 | = 236 |

| hundreds | tens | ones | |
|----------|------|------|--------|
| 1 | 4 | 9 | = 149 |

| | hundreds | tens | ones | total |
|---|----------|------|------|-------|
| 3 hundreds + 4 tens + 8 ones = | 3 | 4 | 8 | = _____ |
| _ hundreds + _ tens + _ ones = | 2 | 1 | 7 | = _____ |
| _ hundreds + _ tens + _ ones = | 6 | 3 | 5 | = _____ |
| _ hundreds + _ tens + _ ones = | 4 | 7 | 9 | = _____ |
| _ hundreds + _ tens + _ ones = | 2 | 9 | 4 | = _____ |
| _ hundreds + 5 tens + 6 ones = | 4 | ____ | ____ | = _____ |
| 3 hundreds + 1 tens + 3 ones = | ____ | ____ | | = _____ |
| 3 hundreds + _ tens + 7 ones = | ____ | 5 | ____ | = _____ |
| 6 hundreds + 2 tens + _ ones = | ____ | ____ | 8 | = _____ |

# Addition: 3-Digit Regrouping

**Directions:** Study the example. Follow the steps to add. Regroup when needed.

**Step 1:** Add the ones.
**Step 2:** Add the tens.
**Step 3:** Add the hundreds.

| hundreds | tens | ones |
|:---:|:---:|:---:|
| 1 | 1 | |
| 3 | 4 | 8 |
| + 4 | 5 | 4 |
| 8 | 0 | 2 |

$10 = 1 \text{ ten} + 0 \text{ ones}$

$$
\begin{array}{r} 348 \\ +214 \\ \hline \end{array}
\qquad
\begin{array}{r} 172 \\ +418 \\ \hline \end{array}
\qquad
\begin{array}{r} 575 \\ +329 \\ \hline \end{array}
\qquad
\begin{array}{r} 623 \\ +268 \\ \hline \end{array}
\qquad
\begin{array}{r} 369 \\ +533 \\ \hline \end{array}
\qquad
\begin{array}{r} 733 \\ +229 \\ \hline \end{array}
$$

$$
\begin{array}{r} 411 \\ +299 \\ \hline \end{array}
\qquad
\begin{array}{r} 423 \\ +169 \\ \hline \end{array}
\qquad
\begin{array}{r} 639 \\ +177 \\ \hline \end{array}
\qquad
\begin{array}{r} 624 \\ +368 \\ \hline \end{array}
\qquad
\begin{array}{r} 272 \\ +469 \\ \hline \end{array}
\qquad
\begin{array}{r} 393 \\ +418 \\ \hline \end{array}
$$

Name _____

# Addition: 3-Digit Regrouping

**Directions:** Study the example. Follow the steps to subtract.

**Step 1:** Regroup ones.
**Step 2:** Subtract ones.
**Step 3:** Subtract tens.
**Step 4:** Subtract hundreds.

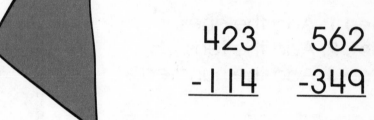

$$423 \quad\quad 562$$
$$-114 \quad\quad -349$$

**Example:**

| hundreds | tens | ones |
|---|---|---|
|  | 5 | 12 |
| 4 | 6̸ | 1̸2̸ |
| -2 | 5 | 3 |
| 2 | 0 | 9 |

$$478 \quad\quad 651$$
$$-239 \quad\quad -333$$

**Directions:** Draw a line to the correct answer. Color the kites.

$$347 \quad 144 \quad 963 \quad 762 \quad 287 \quad 427$$
$$-218 \quad -135 \quad -748 \quad -553 \quad -179 \quad -398$$

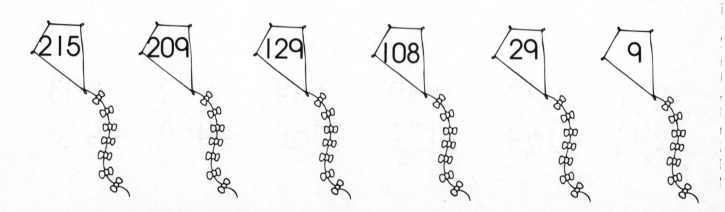

215   209   129   108   29   9

# Graphs: How Many?

**Directions:** Use the chart to help you answer the questions below. Then, graph your results by coloring in the circles for each ball.

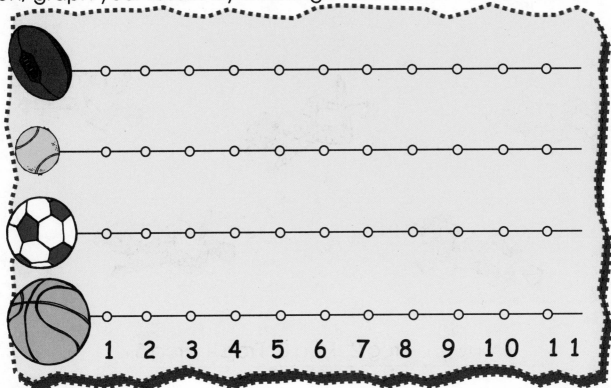

How many did you find?

_____ footballs          _____ soccer balls

_____ tennis balls       _____ basketballs

# Graphs: Frog Bubbles

**Directions:** Complete the line graph to show how many bubbles each frog blew.

How many bubbles? Frog 1:_____  2:_____  3:_____  4:_____  5:_____

Which frog blew the most bubbles?_____

Which frog blew the fewest? _____

# Numbers: Less Than, Greater Than

**Directions:** The open mouth points to the larger number. The small point goes to the smaller number. Draw the symbol < or > to the correct number.

**Example:**

5 ( > ) 3    This means that 5 is greater than 3, and 3 is less than 5.

12 ◯ 2          16 ◯ 6

16 ◯ 15          1 ◯ 2

7 ◯ 1          19 ◯ 5

9 ◯ 6          11 ◯ 13

# Tables: Superstar Second Graders

**Directions:** Complete the table using the information shown. Then, answer the questions.

| Class | Boys | Girls | Total |
|-------|------|-------|-------|
| A | | 17 | 28 |
| B | 12 | 15 | |
| C | 9 | | 23 |
| Total | | | |

Great Job!

1. Which class has the most students?_____

2. Which class has the fewest students?_____

3. How many more girls than boys are in the second grade?_____

4. Which class has the most boys?_____

5. Which class has the fewest girls?_____

6. How many students are in second grade at Superstar School?_____

7. How many more students are in class A than class C?_____

# Fractions: Half, Third, Fourth

**Directions:** Color the correct fraction of each shape.

**Examples:**

shaded part   1
equal parts   2
$\frac{1}{2}$ (one-half)

shaded part   1
equal parts   3
$\frac{1}{3}$ (one-third)

shaded part   1
equal parts   4
$\frac{1}{4}$ (one-fourth)

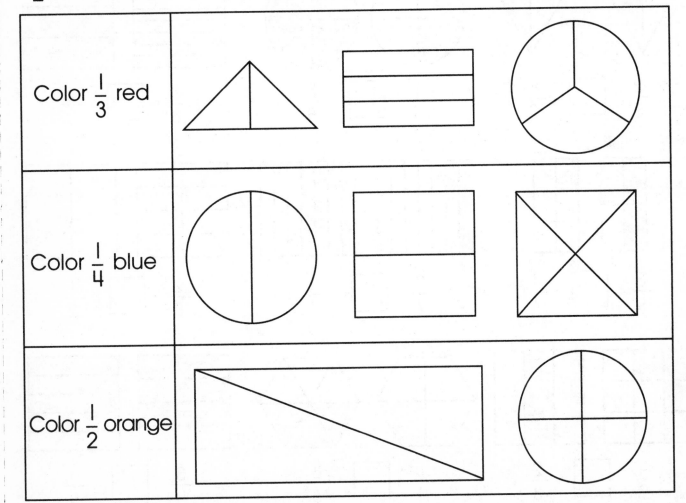

| | |
|---|---|
| Color $\frac{1}{3}$ red | |
| Color $\frac{1}{4}$ blue | |
| Color $\frac{1}{2}$ orange | |

# Fractions: All Shapes and Sizes

**Directions:** Compare the fractions below. Write **<** or **>** in each box.

**Examples:**

$$\frac{2}{4} \boxed{<} \frac{3}{4}$$
less than

$$\frac{3}{4} \boxed{>} \frac{2}{4}$$
greater than

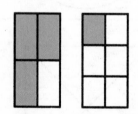

$$\frac{2}{3} \boxed{\phantom{<}} \frac{1}{3}$$

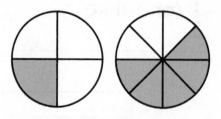

$$\frac{1}{4} \boxed{\phantom{<}} \frac{5}{8}$$

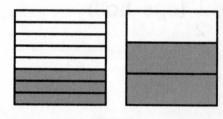

$$\frac{3}{8} \boxed{\phantom{<}} \frac{2}{3}$$

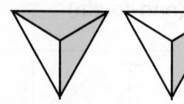

$$\frac{3}{4} \boxed{\phantom{<}} \frac{1}{6}$$

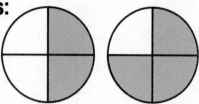

$$\frac{2}{7} \boxed{\phantom{<}} \frac{4}{7}$$

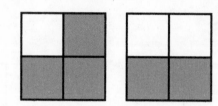

$$\frac{2}{8} \boxed{\phantom{<}} \frac{1}{2}$$

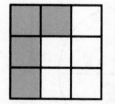

$$\frac{4}{9} \boxed{\phantom{<}} \frac{2}{3}$$

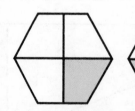

$$\frac{1}{4} \boxed{\phantom{<}} \frac{3}{6}$$

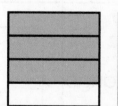

$$\frac{3}{4} \boxed{\phantom{<}} \frac{4}{5}$$

Name _____

# Fractions: Fun With Fractions

4 gloves are shaded. 9 gloves in all.

$\frac{4}{9}$ of the gloves are shaded.

**Directions:** Look at the picture of the toys. Answer the questions below.

What fraction of the balls is shaded? _____

cars? _____          trains? _____

dolls? _____          airplanes? _____

teddy bears? _____   rabbits? _____

hats? _____          boats? _____

# Fractions: Problem Solving

A fraction is a number that names part of a whole, such as $\frac{1}{2}$ or $\frac{1}{3}$.

**Directions:** Read each problem. Use the pictures to help you solve the problem. Write the fraction that answers the question.

Simon and Jessie shared a pizza.
Together they ate $\frac{3}{4}$ of the pizza.
How much of the pizza is left? _____

Sylvia baked a cherry pie. She gave $\frac{1}{3}$
to her grandmother and $\frac{1}{3}$ to a friend.
How much of the pie did she keep? _____

Timmy erased $\frac{1}{2}$ of the blackboard
before the bell rang for recess.
How much of the blackboard does he
have left to erase? _____

**Directions:** Read the problem. Draw your own picture to help you solve the problem. Write the fraction that answers the question.

Sarah mowed $\frac{1}{4}$ of the yard before lunch.
How much does she have left to mow? _____

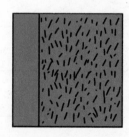

Name _____

# Geometry

Geometry is mathematics that has to do with lines and shapes.

**Directions:** Color the shapes.

**Color** the triangles blue.
**Color** the circles red.
**Color** the squares green.
**Color** the rectangles pink.

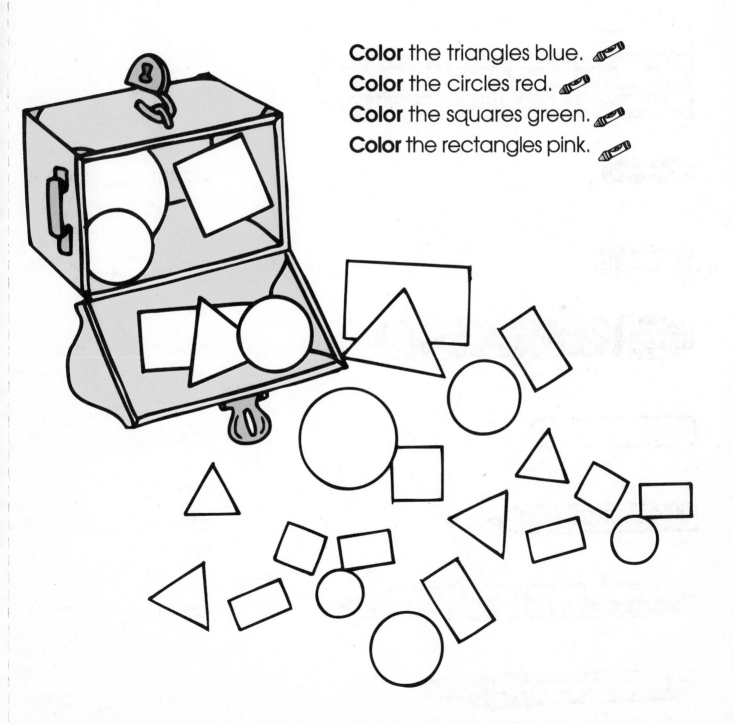

# Estimating: Inches

An inch is a unit of length in the standard measurement system.

**Directions:** Use a ruler to measure each object to the nearest inch.

I inch

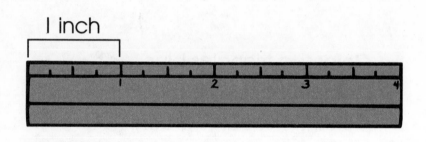

about __1__ inches

about ____ inches

about ____ inches

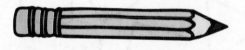

about ____ inches

about ____ inches

about ____ inches

about ____ inches

# Telling Time: Hour, Half-Hour

An hour is sixty minutes. The short hand of a clock tells the hour. It is written **0:00**, such as **5:00**. A half-hour is thirty minutes. When the long hand of the clock is pointing to the six, the time is on the half-hour. It is written **:30**, such as **5:30**.

**Directions:** Study the examples. Tell what time it is on each clock.

**Examples:**

 9:00

The minute hand is on the 12.
The hour hand is on the 9.
It is 9 o'clock.

 4:30

The minute hand is on the 6.
The hour hand is *between* 4 and 5.
It is 4:30.

____　____　____　____　____

____　____　____　____　____

# Telling Time: Quarter-Hours

Time can also be shown as fractions. 30 minutes = $\frac{1}{2}$ hour.

**Directions:** Shade the fraction of each clock and tell how many minutes you have shaded.

**Example:**

$\frac{1}{2}$ hour

$\underline{30}$ minutes

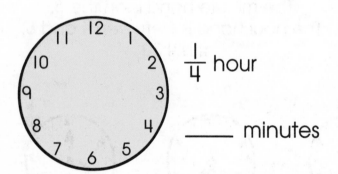

$\frac{1}{4}$ hour

_____ minutes

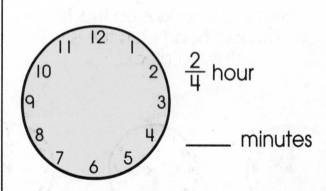

$\frac{2}{4}$ hour

_____ minutes

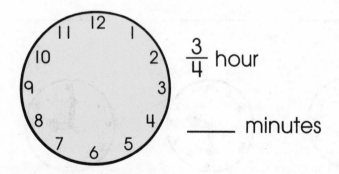

$\frac{3}{4}$ hour

_____ minutes

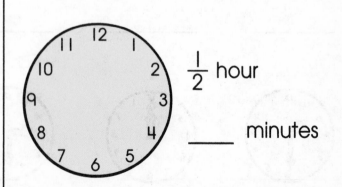

$\frac{1}{2}$ hour

_____ minutes

# Telling Time: Problem Solving

**Directions:** Solve each problem.

Tracy wakes up at 7:00. She has 30 minutes before her bus comes. What time does her bus come?

___ : _____

Vera walks her dog for 15 minutes after supper. She finishes supper at 6:30. When does she get home from walking her dog?

___ : _____

Chip practices the piano for 30 minutes when he gets home from school. He gets home at 3:30. When does he stop practicing?

___ : _____

Tanya starts mowing the grass at 4:30. She finishes at 5:00. For how many minutes does she mow the lawn?

_____ minutes

Don does his homework for 45 minutes. He starts his work at 7:15. When does he stop working?

___ : _____

# Telling Time: Time to Play Ball

**Directions:** Write the number of the matching clock in front of each sentence.

1.
2.
3.

4.
5.
6.

7.
8.
9.
10.

_____ Mary's coach says she should be in bed by 9:30 P.M. the night before a game.

_____ Tom's baseball team practices at 6:15 P.M.

_____ It was 6:08 P.M. when Mike arrived at practice.

_____ Coach told the team their next game was tomorrow at 4:45 P.M.

_____ The National Anthem was played over the loudspeaker at 4:35 P.M.

_____ Steve and Paul pitch to each other every day at 3:35.

_____ Emily went to see her friend Sue's game at 10:21 A.M.

_____ Coach had us practice running the bases at 2:37 P.M.

_____ Our game was rained out at 5:51 P.M.

_____ Sue's game was finished at 12:09 P.M.

# Money: Penny, Nickel, Dime

Penny **1¢**        Nickel **5¢**        Dime **10¢**

**Directions:** Count the coins and write the amount.

    ___16___ ¢

    _____ ¢            _____ ¢

    _____ ¢            _____ ¢

Name _____

# Money: Quarter

A quarter is worth 25¢.

**Directions:** Count the coins and write the amounts.

 _____ ¢

 _____ ¢

 _____ ¢

 _____ ¢

 _____ ¢

 _____ ¢

 _____ ¢

 _____ ¢

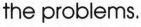

# Money: Problem Solving

**Directions:** Read each problem. Use the pictures to help you solve the problems.

Ben bought a ball. He had 11¢ left.
How much money did he have at the start?          _____ ¢

Tara has 75¢. She buys a car.
How much money does she have left?          _____ ¢

Leah wants to buy a doll and a ball. She has 80¢.
How much more money does she need?          _____ ¢

Jacob has 95¢. He buys the car and the ball.
How much more money does he need to
buy a doll for his sister?          _____ ¢

Kim paid three quarters, one dime
and three pennies for a hat.
How much did it cost?          _____ ¢

# Money: Dollar

One dollar equals 100 cents. It is written $1.00.

**Directions:** Count the money and write the amounts.

  $____.____

  $____.____

  $____.____

  $____.____

  $____.____

  $____.____

  $____.____

  $____.____

Name _____

# Money: Review

**Directions:** Add the money and write the total.

  _____ ¢

  _____ ¢

  $___.____

  _____ ¢

  $___.____

# Multiplication: Multiplying Creatures

Multiplication is a short way to find the sum of adding the same number a certain amount of times. For example, **7 x 4 = 28** instead of **7 + 7 + 7 + 7 = 28**.

**Directions:** Study the example. Solve the problems.

**Example:**

3 + 3 + 3 = 9
3 threes = 9
3 x 3 = 9

7 + 7 = 14
2 sevens = 14
2 x 7 = 14

4 + 4 + 4 + 4 = ____
4 fours = ____
4 x ____ = ____

5 + 5 = ____
2 fives = ____
2 x ____ = ____

2 + 2 + 2 + 2 = ____
4 twos = ____
4 x ____ = ____

6 + 6 = ____
2 sixes = ____
2 x ____ = ____

# Multiplication: Drawing Groups

Multiplication is repeated addition.

**Directions:** Draw a picture for each problem.
Then write the missing numbers.

**Example:**

Draw 2 groups of three apples.

$3 + 3 = 6$

or $2 \times 3 = 6$

| Draw 3 groups of four hearts. | Draw 2 groups of five boxes. |
|---|---|
|  $4 + 4 + 4 = $ ____  <br> or $3 \times$ ____ $= $ ____ | $5 + $ ____ $= $ ____ <br> or $2 \times$ ____ $= $ ____ |

Draw 6 groups of two circles.

$2 + $ ___ $+$ ___ $+$ ___ $+$ ___ $+$ ___ $= $ ___

or $6 \times$ ___ $= $ ____

Draw 7 groups of three triangles.

$3 + $ ___ $+$ ___ $+$ ___ $+$ ___ $+$ ___ $+$ ___ $= $ ___

or ____ $\times$ ____ $= $ ____

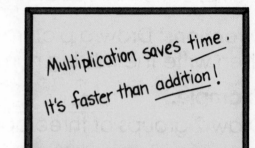

Multiplication saves time. It's faster than addition!

# Multiplication: Review

**Directions:** Solve the problems.

$9 + 9 = \underline{18}$

2 nines = \_\_\_\_

$2 \times 9 = $ \_\_\_\_

$7 + 7 = $ \_\_\_\_

2 sevens = \_\_\_\_

$2 \times \underline{7} = $ \_\_\_\_

$4 + 4 + 4 + 4 = $ \_\_\_\_

$\underline{4}$ fours = \_\_\_\_

\_\_\_\_ $\times 4 = $ \_\_\_\_

$8 + 8 + 8 + 8 + 8 = $ \_\_\_\_

\_\_\_\_ eights = \_\_\_\_

\_\_\_\_ $\times 8 = $ \_\_\_\_

$5 + 5 + 5 = $ \_\_\_\_

\_\_\_\_ fives = \_\_\_\_

\_\_\_\_ $\times 5 = $ \_\_\_\_

$9 + 9 = $ \_\_\_\_

\_\_\_\_ nines = \_\_\_\_

\_\_\_\_ $\times 9 = $ \_\_\_\_

$6 + 6 + 6 = $ \_\_\_\_

\_\_\_\_ sixes = \_\_\_\_

\_\_\_\_ $\times 6 = $ \_\_\_\_

$3 + 3 = $ \_\_\_\_

\_\_\_\_ threes = \_\_\_\_

\_\_\_\_ $\times 3 = $ \_\_\_\_

$7 + 7 + 7 + 7 = $ \_\_\_\_

\_\_\_\_ sevens = \_\_\_\_

\_\_\_\_ $\times 7 = $ \_\_\_\_

$2 + 2 = $ \_\_\_\_

\_\_\_\_ twos = \_\_\_\_

\_\_\_\_ $\times 2 = $ \_\_\_\_

# Sound Spelling Review: Long and Short Vowels

**Directions:** Read the words in each box. Cross out the word that does not belong.

| long vowels | short vowels |
|---|---|
| cube | man |
| cup | pet |
| rake | fix |
| me | ice |
| long vowels | short vowels |
| soap | cat |
| seed | pin |
| read | rain |
| mat | frog |

**Directions:** Write **short** or **long** to label the words in each box.

| _____ vowels | _____ vowels |
|---|---|
| hose | frog |
| take | hot |
| bead | sled |
| cube | lap |
| eat | block |
| see | sit |

# Tricky Sound Spellings: R-Controlled Vowels

When a vowel is followed by the letter **r**, it has a different sound.

**Example: he** and **her**

**Directions:** Write a word from the word box to finish each sentence. Notice the sound of the vowel followed by an **r**.

| | | | | |
|---|---|---|---|---|
| park | chair | horse | bark | bird |
| hurt | girl | hair | store | ears |

1. A dog likes to _____.

2. You buy food at a _____.

3. Children like to play at the _____.

4. An animal you can ride is a _____.

5. You hear with your _____.

6. A robin is a kind of _____.

7. If you fall down, you might get _____.

8. The opposite of a boy is a _____.

9. You comb and brush your _____.

10. You sit down on a _____.

# Tricky Sound Spellings: ou, ow, au, aw

The vowel teams **ou** and **ow** can have the same sound. You can hear it in the words **clown** and **cloud**. The vowel teams **au** and **aw** have the same sound. You hear it in the words **because** and **law**.

**Directions:** Look at the pictures. Write the correct vowel team to complete the words. The first one is done for you. You may need to use a dictionary to help you with the correct spelling.

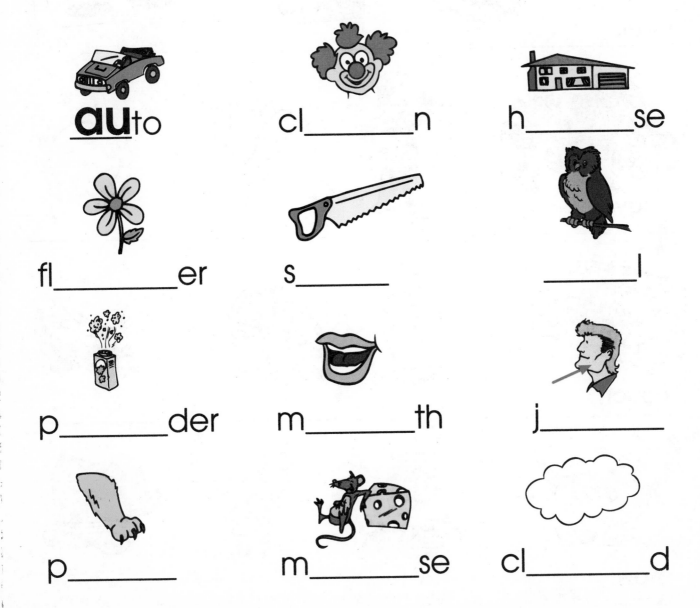

**au**to

cl_____n

h_____se

fl_____er

s_____

_____l

p_____der

m_____th

j_____

p_____

m_____se

cl_____d

# Tricky Sound Spellings: oi, oy, ou, ow

**Directions:** Look at the first picture in each row. Circle the pictures that have the same sound.

**oil**

**toy**

**couch**

**howl**

# Tricky Sound Spellings: Consonant Blends

**Blends** are 2 or 3 consonant letters whose sounds combine, or blend, in a word, such as **tr** in **tree**.

**Directions:** Fill in the circle beside the missing blend in each word.

| __ain | __an | te__ |
|---|---|---|
| ○ sk | ○ sl | ○ sk |
| ○ tr | ○ sm | ○ nt |
| ○ pr | ○ sw | ○ ng |
| __ate | __ate | __ide |
| ○ sk | ○ pl | ○ sk |
| ○ sm | ○ pr | ○ cl |
| ○ cr | ○ sp | ○ sl |
| __ail | __ess | de__ |
| ○ ng | ○ pr | ○ st |
| ○ sn | ○ dr | ○ nd |
| ○ st | ○ nd | ○ sk |

# Tricky Sound Spellings: ch, sh, th, wh

**Directions:** Fill in the circle beside the missing sound in each word.

| | | |
|---|---|---|
| **_ale** | **pea_** | **_ain** |
| ○ wh | ○ ck | ○ kn |
| ○ wr | ○ th | ○ ch |
| ○ ch | ○ ch | ○ wr |
| **_imp** | **_ell** | **_eel** |
| ○ ck | ○ ch | ○ ck |
| ○ kn | ○ sh | ○ wh |
| ○ ch | ○ ck | ○ kn |
| **too_** | **fi_** | **_orn** |
| ○ kn | ○ ch | ○ th |
| ○ wr | ○ sh | ○ wr |
| ○ th | ○ th | ○ ch |

# Tricky Sound Spellings: Silent Letters

Some words have letters you can't hear at all, such as the **gh** in **night**, the **w** in **wrong**, the **l** in **walk**, the **k** in **knee**, the **b** in **climb**, and the **t** in **listen**.

**Directions:** Look at the words in the word box. Write the word under its picture. Underline the silent letters.

| knife | light | calf | wrench | lamb | eight |
|-------|-------|------|--------|------|-------|
| wrist | whistle | comb | thumb | knob | knee |

_____ _____ _____ _____

_____ _____ _____ _____

 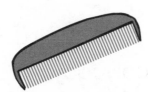  

_____ _____ _____ _____

Name _____

# Contractions

**Directions:** Match the words with their contractions.

would not            I've

was not             he'll

he will             wouldn't

could not            wasn't

I have              couldn't

**Directions:** Make the words at the end of each line into contractions to complete the sentences.

1. He _____ know the answer.          **did not**

2. _____ a long way home.           **It is**

3. _____ my house.              **Here is**

4. _____ not going to school today.      **We are**

5. _____ take the bus home tomorrow.     **They will**

# Compound Words

**Compound words** are formed by putting together two smaller words.

**Directions:** Help the cook brew her stew. Mix words from the first column with words from the second column to make new words. Write your new words on the lines at the bottom.

| | |
|---|---|
| grand | brows |
| snow | light |
| eye | stairs |
| down | string |
| rose | book |
| shoe | mother |
| note | ball |
| moon | bud |

1. _____

2. _____

3. _____

4. _____

5. _____

6. _____

7. _____

8. _____

# Compound Words

**Directions:** Draw a line under the compound word in each sentence. On the line, write the two words that make up the compound word.

1. A firetruck came to help put out the fire.

_____

2. I will be nine years old on my next birthday.

_____

3. We built a treehouse at the back.

_____

4. Dad put a scarecrow in his garden.

_____

5. It is fun to make footprints in the snow.

_____

6. I like to read the comics in the newspaper.

_____

7. Cowboys ride horses and use lassos.

_____

# Synonyms

**Synonyms** are words that have almost the same meaning.

**Directions:** Read the story. Then fill in the blanks with the synonyms.

| funny | unhappy |
|-------|---------|
| windy | little  |

**A New Balloon**

It was a breezy day. The wind blew the small child's balloon away. The child was sad. A silly clown gave him a new balloon.

1. It was a _____ day.

2. The wind blew the _____ child's balloon away.

3. The child was _____ .

4. A _____ clown gave him a new balloon.

# Antonyms

**Antonyms** are words that mean the opposite of another word.

**Examples:**
 **hot** and **cold**
 **short** and **tall**

**Directions:** Draw a line from each word on the left to its antonym on the right.

| | |
|---|---|
| sad | white |
| bottom | stop |
| black | fat |
| tall | top |
| thin | hard |
| little | found |
| cold | short |
| lost | hot |
| go | big |
| soft | happy |

# Homophones

**Homophones** are words that sound the same but have different spellings and meanings, such as **see** and **sea**.

**Directions:** Match each word with its homophone.

| | |
|---|---|
| eight | blew |
| buy | whole |
| pail | ate |
| red | pale |
| hole | read |
| blue | hour |
| our | by |

**Directions:** Choose 3 homophone pairs and write sentences using them.

1. _____

2. _____

3. _____

# Syllables

Words are made up of parts called **syllables**. Each syllable has a vowel sound. One way to count syllables is to clap as you say the word.

**Example:**
| | | |
|---|---|---|
| cat | 1 clap | 1 syllable |
| table | 2 claps | 2 syllables |
| butterfly | 3 claps | 3 syllables |

**Direction:** "Clap out" the words below. Write how many syllables each word has.

| | | | |
|---|---|---|---|
| movie | _____ | dog | _____ |
| piano | _____ | basket | _____ |
| tree | _____ | swimmer | _____ |
| bicycle | _____ | rainbow | _____ |
| sun | _____ | paper | _____ |
| cabinet | _____ | picture | _____ |
| football | _____ | run | _____ |
| television | _____ | enter | _____ |

# Prefixes

**Directions:** Change the meaning of the sentences by adding the prefixes to the **bold** words.

The boy was **lucky** because he guessed the answer **correctly**.

The boy was (un) _____ because he guessed the

answer (in) _____ .

When Mary **behaved**, she felt **happy**.

When Mary (mis) _____ ,

she felt (un) _____ .

Mike wore his jacket **buttoned** because the dance was **formal**.

Mike wore his jacket (un) _____ because the dance

was (in) _____ .

Tim **understood** because he was **familiar** with the book.

Tim (mis) _____ because he was

(un) _____ with the book.

# Suffixes

Adding **ing** to the end of a word means that it is happening now.
Adding **ed** to the end of a word means it happened in the past.

**Directions:** Look at the words in the word box. Underline the root word in each one. Write a word to complete each sentence.

| | | | | |
|---|---|---|---|---|
| snowing | wished | played | looking | crying |
| talking | walked | eating | going | doing |

1. We like to play. We _____ yesterday.

2. Is that snow? Yes, it is _____.

3. Do you want to go with me? No, I am _____ with my friend.

4. The baby will cry if we leave. The baby is _____.

5. We will walk home from school. We _____ to school this morning.

6. Did you wish for a new bike? Yes, I _____ for one.

7. Who is going to do it while we are away? I am _____ it.

8. Did you talk to your friend? Yes, we are _____ now.

9. Will you look at my book? I am _____ at it now.

10. I like to eat pizza. We are _____ it today.

Name _____

# Building a Sentence: Nouns

A **noun** is the name of a person, place, or thing.

Directions: Read the story and circle all the nouns. Then write the nouns next to the pictures below.

Our family likes to go to the park.

_____

We play on the swings.

_____

We eat cake.

_____

We drink lemonade.

_____

We throw the ball to our dog.

_____

Then we go home.

_____

# Building a Sentence: Proper Nouns

**Proper nouns** are the names of specific people, places, and pets.
**Proper nouns** begin with a capital letter.

Directions: Write capital letters where they should appear in the sentences below.

**Example:** joe can play in january.

Joe can play in January.

1. we celebrate thanksgiving on the fourth thursday in november.

_____

_____

2. in june, michelle and mark will go camping every friday.

_____

_____

3. on mondays in october, i will take piano lessons.

_____

_____

# Building a Sentence: Adjectives

**Adjectives** are words that tell more about a person, place, or thing.

**Examples:** cold, fuzzy, dark

**Directions:** Think of your own adjectives. Write a story about Fluffy the cat.

1. Fluffy is a _____ cat.

2. The color of his fur is _____ .

3. He likes to chew on my _____ shoes.

4. He likes to eat _____ cat food.

5. I like Fluffy because he is so _____ .

# Building a Sentence: Pronouns

**Pronouns** are words that can be used instead of nouns. **She**, **he**, **it**, and **they** are pronouns.

Directions: Read the sentence. Then write the sentence again, using **she**, **he**, **it**, or **they** in the blank.

1. Dan likes funny jokes. _____ likes funny jokes.

2. Peg and Sam went to the zoo. _____ went to the zoo.

3. My dog likes to dig in the yard. _____ likes to dig in the yard.

4. Sara is a very good dancer. _____ is a very good dancer.

5. Fred and Ted are twins. _____ are twins.

# Building a Sentence: Ownership

We add **'s** to nouns (people, places, or things) to tell who or what owns something.

**Directions:** Read the sentences. Fill in the blanks to show ownership.

**Example:** The doll belongs to **Sara**.
It is **Sara's** doll.

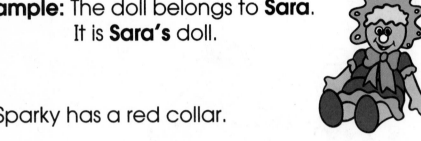

1. Sparky has a red collar.

_____ collar is red.

2. Jimmy has a blue coat.

_____ coat is blue.

3. The tail of the cat is short.

The _____ tail is short.

4. The name of my mother is Karen.

My _____ name is Karen.

# Building a Sentence: Verbs

We use **verbs** to tell when something happens. Sometimes we add an **ed** to verbs that tell us if something has already happened.

**Example:** Today, we will **play**. Yesterday, we **played**.

Directions: Write the correct verb in the blank.

1. Today, I will _____ my dog, Fritz.
   wash      washed

2. Last week, Fritz _____ when we said, "Bath time, Fritz."
   cry      cried

3. My sister likes to _____ wash Fritz.
   help      helped

4. One time she _____ Fritz by herself.
   clean      cleaned

5. Fritz will _____ a lot better after his bath.
   look      looked

# Building a Sentence: Verbs

**Directions:** Write each verb in the correct column.

| rake | talked | look | hopped | skip |
| cooked | fished | call | clean | sewed |

### Yesterday

_____

_____

_____

_____

_____

### Today

_____

_____

_____

_____

_____

# Building a Sentence: Location Words

**Directions:** Use a location word to tell where the cat is in each sentence.

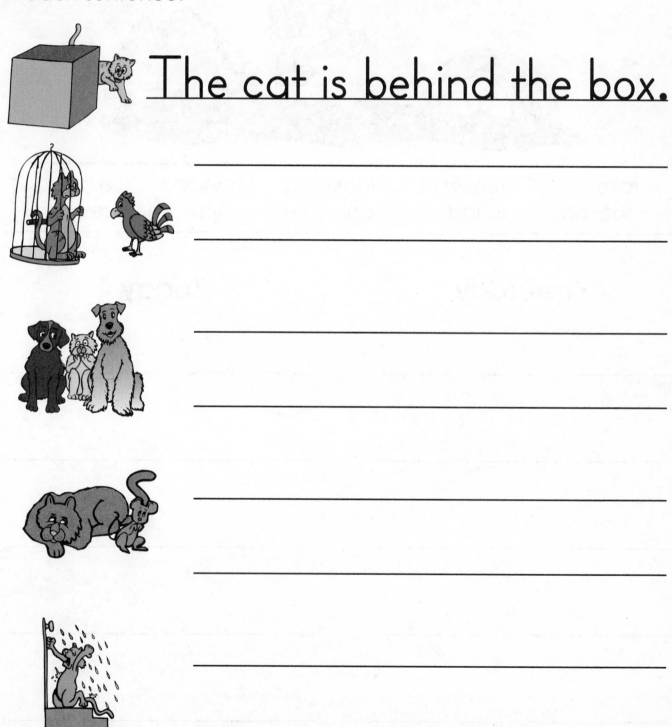

The cat is behind the box.

# Building a Sentence: Subject and Predicate

The **subject** part of the sentence is the person, place, or thing the sentence is about. The **predicate** is the part of the sentence that tells what the subject does.

**Directions:** Draw a line between the subject and the predicate. Underline the noun in the subject and circle the verb.

**Example:**   The furry <u>cat</u> | (ate) food.

1. Mandi walks to school.

2. The bus driver drove the children.

3. The school bell rang very loudly.

4. The teacher spoke to the students.

5. The girls opened their books.

# Sentences and Non-Sentences

A **sentence** tells a complete idea. It has a subject and a predicate. It begins with a capital letter and has punctuation at the end.

**Directions:** Circle the group of words if it is a sentence.

1. Grass is a green plant.

2. Mowing the lawn.

3. Grass grows in fields and lawns.

4. Tickle the feet.

5. Sheep, cows, and horses eat grass.

6. We like to play in.

7. My sister likes to mow the lawn.

8. A picnic on the grass.

9. My dog likes to roll in the grass.

10. Planting flowers around.

# Reading for Sequence

**Directions:** Read about making clay. Then follow the instructions.

It is fun to work with clay. Here is what you need to make it:

1 cup salt

2 cups flour

3/4 cup water

Mix the salt and flour. Then add the water. DO NOT eat the clay. It tastes bad. Use your hands to mix and mix. Now, roll it out. What can you make with your clay?

1. Circle the main idea:

Do not eat clay.

Mix salt, flour, and water to make clay.

2. Write the steps for making clay.

a. _____

b. _____

c. Mix the clay.

d. _____

3. Write why you should not eat clay. _____

_____

# Reading for Sequence

Mrs. Posey made a new hat, but she forgot how she did it. When she tried to tell her friend, she got all mixed up.

**Directions:** Read Mrs. Posey's story. Write her story on the lines in the order you think it happened. Then color the picture.

I glued flowers on it. Then I bought this straw hat. Now, I am wearing my hat. Then I added ribbon around the flowers. I tried on many hats at the store.

The real story:

_____

_____

_____

_____

_____

_____

_____

_____

# Reading for Context Clues

**Directions:** Read the story. Use context clues to figure out the missing words. Write the words from the word box. Then, answer the questions.

| socks | scarf | sweaters | mittens |

Maria bundles up. She sticks her arms through

_____

two _____. She tugs three pairs of

_____

_____ over her feet. She wraps a _____

around her neck. At last, she pulls her _____

onto her hands. Maria goes outside to play. Nobody is warmer

than Maria.

1. What clue words helped you figure out sweaters?

_____

_____

2. What clue words helped you figure out mittens?

_____

_____

# Reading for Context Clues

**Directions:** Read the clues carefully. Then, number the cats. When you are sure you are correct, color the cats.

1. A gray cat sits on the gate.

2. A cat with orange and black spots sits near the tree.

3. A brown cat sits near the bush.

4. A white cat sits between the orange and black spotted cat and the gray cat.

5. A black cat sits next to the brown cat.

6. An orange cat sits between the gray cat and the black cat.

Name _____

# Reading for Plot and Setting

Stories have a setting and a plot. The **setting** tells where and when the story takes place. The **plot** tells what happened.

**Directions:** Read the story. Then, follow the directions below.

Michael, Sam, and Dominic were best friends. They ate lunch together. At recess, they swung on the swings together. On the swings, Michael said, "Come to my house to play after school."

Dominic thought Michael was looking at Sam. He waited for Michael to ask him, too, but Michael didn't. All afternoon, Dominic felt sad. When the bell rang, he started to go home. "Where are you going?" Michael called. "I wanted you both to come to my house." With a big smile, Dominic ran to join Michael and Sam.

Fill in the circle beside the words that tell about the story's setting.

- ◯ After school at Sam's house
- ◯ At school on a school day
- ◯ At the park on a Saturday

Number the plot events to show the order in which they happened.

☐ Dominic felt sad because he thought he wasn't invited.

☐ Dominic and Sam went to Michael's house.

☐ Michael invited the boys over.

# Reading for Details

**Directions:** Read the story. Then answer the questions.

Sometimes Marvin and Mugsy scratch and itch. Marcy knows that fleas or ticks are insect pests to her pets. Their bites are painful. Fleas suck the blood of animals. They don't have wings, but they can jump. Ticks are very flat, suck blood, and are related to spiders. They like to hide in dogs' ears. That is why Marcy checks Marvin and Mugsy every week for fleas and ticks.

1. What is a pest? _____

_____

2. List three facts about fleas.

   1) _____

   2) _____

   3) _____

3. List three facts about ticks.

   1) _____

   2) _____

   3) _____

# Reading for Main Ideas

**Directions:** Read the story. Then answer the questions.

Tonda has many books. She gets different ideas from these books. Some of her books are about fish. Some are about cardboard and paper crafts. Some are about nature. Others are about reusing junk. Tonda wants to make a paper airplane. She reads about it in one of her books. Then she asks an adult to help her.

1. Circle the main idea:

   Tonda learns about different ideas from books.

   Tonda likes crafts.

2. (Circle the correct answer.) Tonda is:

   a person who likes to read.

   a person who doesn't like books.

3. What does Tonda want to make from paper? _____

   _____

4. Write two ways to learn how to do something.

   1) _____

   2) _____

Name _____

# Reading for Main Ideas

**Directions:** Read the story. Then follow the instructions.

Angela learned a lot about sharks when her class visited the city aquarium. She learned that sharks are fish. Some sharks are as big as an elephant, and some can fit into a small paper bag. Sharks have no bones. They have hundreds of teeth, and when they lose them, they grow new ones. They eat animals of any kind. Whale sharks are the largest of all fish.

1. Circle the main idea:

   Angela learned a lot about sharks at the aquarium.

   Some sharks are as big as elephants.

2. When sharks lose teeth, they _____

   _____ .

3. _____ are the largest of all fish.

4. Sharks have bones. (Circle the answer.)

   Yes                    No

**Summer Link Basic Learning Skills Grade 3**          74

# Reading for Main Ideas

Samantha thought of a good joke. She bragged that she could read Maria's mind. She put her hand on Maria's head, closed her eyes, and said, "You had red punch with your lunch!"

"Wow! You're right!" replied Maria, not realizing that she had a little red ring around her lips.

"That was easy. But I bet you can't tell me what I just ate," said Thomas.

"That's a bunch of baloney," answered Samantha.

"How did you know?" gasped Thomas.

"It's my little secret," said Samantha, with a sigh of relief.

"Here comes your mom," said Maria. "Can you read her mind, too?"

Samantha looked down at her watch. She should have been home half an hour ago. As she ran to meet her mother, she yelled back, "Yes, I know exactly what she's thinking!"

**Directions:** Make inferences about Samantha's mind-reading tricks. Fill in the circle beside the correct inference.

1. Was Samantha sure that Thomas had eaten bologna for lunch?

   ○ No, she was just lucky.

   ○ Yes, she saw him eat his bologna sandwich.

2. What was Samantha's mother probably thinking?

   ○ Samantha was a great mind reader.

   ○ Samantha was late.

">

Name _____

# Reading for Cause and Effect

Things that happen can make other things happen. The event that happens is the **effect**. Why the event happens is the **cause**.

**Example:** Marcie tripped on the step and fell down.
   **Cause:** Marcie tripped on the step.
   **Effect:** Marcie fell down.

**Directions:** Read the story.

Marcie knows a magic trick. She can make a ring seem to go up and down by itself on a pencil. Marcie has to get ready ahead of time. She ties a piece of skinny thread under the pencil's eraser. Then, she ties the thread to a button on her blouse. In front of her audience, Marcie puts a ring on the pencil. When Marcie leans forward, the thread goes loose, so the ring goes down. Then, Marcie leans back. The thread tightens and makes the ring go up the pencil.

**Directions:** Write the cause to complete each sentence.

1. The audience cannot see the thread because

   _____

   ------------------------------------------------

   _____

   _____

2. ------------------------------------------------

   _____

   makes the ring go down.

">
Summer Link Basic Learning Skills Grade 3          76

Name _____

# Reading: Predict What Happens

**Directions:** Read the story. Then answer the questions.

Marcy had a great idea for a game to play with her dogs, Marvin and Mugsy. The game was called "Dog Derby." Marcy would stand at one end of the driveway and hold on to the dogs by their collars. Her friend Mitch would stand at the other end of the driveway. When he said, "Go!" Marcy would let go of the dogs and they would race to Mitch. The first one there would get a dog biscuit. If there was a tie, both dogs would get a biscuit.

1. Who do you think will win the race?

_____

Why? _____

_____

2. What do you think will happen when they race again?

_____

_____

Name _____

# Fiction: Made-Up Stories

**Directions: Fiction** is a make-believe story. Read the stories. Underline the sentence that makes each story fiction.

Michelle got a kitten for her birthday. It was soft and cuddly. It liked to chase fuzzy toys. After playing, it napped in Michelle's lap. One day the kitten said to Michelle, "Would you like me to tell you a story?"

The team lined up. The kicker kicked the football. Up, up it soared. It went up so high that it went into orbit around the Earth. The game was over. The Aardvarks had won.

"This is a great car," the salesperson said. "It can go very fast. It can cook your breakfast. It always starts, even on the coldest day. You really should buy this car."

Chris studied about healthy food in school. He learned that milk could make him grow. Chris drank a glass of milk just before he went to bed. When he got up in the morning, he was so tall, his head went right through the ceiling.

# Nonfiction: True Facts

**Directions: Nonfiction** is a true story. Read about tornadoes. Then follow the instructions.

A tornado begins over land with strong winds and thunderstorms. The spinning air becomes a funnel. It can cause damage. If you are inside, go to the lowest floor of the building. A basement is a safe place. A bathroom or closet in the middle of a building can be a safe place, too. If you are outside, lie in a ditch. Remember, tornadoes are dangerous.

Write five facts about tornadoes.

1. _____

    _____

2. _____

    _____

3. _____

    _____

4. _____

    _____

5. _____

    _____

# Fiction or Nonfiction: Which Is It?

**Directions:** Read about fiction and nonfiction books. Then follow the instructions.

There are many kinds of books. Some books have make-believe stories about princesses and dragons. Some books contain poetry and rhymes, like Mother Goose. These are fiction.

Some books contain facts about space and plants. And still other books have stories about famous people in history like Abraham Lincoln. These are nonfiction.

Write **F** for fiction and **NF** for nonfiction.

_____ 1. nursery rhyme

_____ 2. fairy tale

_____ 3. true life story of a famous athlete

_____ 4. Aesop's fables

_____ 5. dictionary entry about foxes

_____ 6. weather report

_____ 7. story about a talking tree

_____ 8. story about how a tadpole becomes a frog

_____ 9. story about animal habitats

_____ 10. riddles and jokes

# Learning Dictionary Skills: ABC Order

If the first letters of two words are the same, look at the second letters in both words. If the second letters are the same, look at the third letters.

**Directions:** Write 1, 2, 3, or 4 on the lines in each row to put the words in ABC order.

**Example:**

1. __1__ candy     __2__ carrot     __4__ duck     __3__ dance

2. _____ cold     _____ hot     _____ carry     _____ hit

3. _____ flash     _____ fan     _____ fun     _____ garden

4. _____ seat     _____ sun     _____ saw     _____ sit

5. _____ row     _____ ring     _____ rock     _____ run

6. _____ truck     _____ turn     _____ twin     _____ talk

7. _____ seven     _____ shoe     _____ soup     _____ smell

Name _____

# Learning Dictionary Skills

**Directions:** Look at this page from a picture dictionary. Then answer the questions.

**safe**

A metal box

**sea**

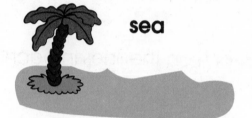

A body of water

**seed**

The beginning of a plant

**sheep**

An animal that has wool

**store**

A place where items are sold

**skate**

A shoe with wheels or a blade on it

**snowstorm**

A time when much snow falls

**squirrel**

A small animal with a bushy tail

**stone**

A small rock

1. What kind of animal has wool? _____

2. What do you call a shoe with wheels on it? _____

3. When a lot of snow falls, what is it called? _____

4. What is a small animal with a bushy tail? _____

5. What is a place where items are sold? _____

6. When a plant starts, what is it called? _____

# Learning Dictionary Skills

When words have more than one meaning, the meanings are numbered in a dictionary.

**Directions:** Read the meanings of **tag**. Write the number of the correct definition after each sentence.

**tag**

1. A small strip or tab attached to something else

2. To label

3. To follow closely and constantly

4. A game of chase

1. We will play a game of tag after we study. _____

2. I will tag this coat with its price. _____

3. My little brother will tag along with us. _____

4. My mother already took off the price tag. _____

5. The tag on the puppy said, "For Sale." _____

6. Do not tag that tree. _____

**Number Knowledge: Finding Patterns**

Mia likes to count by twos, threes, fours, fives, tens, and hundreds.

Directions: Complete the number patterns.

1. 5, **10**, **15**, 20, **25**, **30**, 35, **40**, **45**, 50

2. 100, **200**, **300**, 400, **500**, **600**, **700**, 800, **900**

3. **2**, 4, 6, **8**, **10**, 12, **14**, 16, **18**, **20**

4. 10, **20**, **30**, 40, **50**, **60**, 70, **80**, 90

5. 4, **8**, 12, **16**, **20**, 24, **28**, 32, **36**, 40

6. **3**, 6, 9, **12**, **15**, 18, **21**, 24, 27, 30

Directions: Make up two of your own number patterns.

Answers will vary.

Page 6

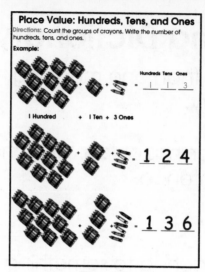

**Place Value: Hundreds, Tens, and Ones**

Directions: Count the groups of crayons. Write the number of hundreds, tens, and ones.

Example:

Hundreds Tens Ones
1   1   3

1 Hundred + 1 Ten + 3 Ones

**1 2 4**

**1 3 6**

Page 7

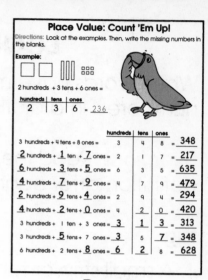

**Place Value: Count 'Em Up!**

Directions: Look at the examples. Then, write the missing numbers in the blanks.

Example:

2 hundreds + 3 tens + 6 =

| hundreds | tens | ones | |
|---|---|---|---|
| 2 | 3 | 6 | = **236** |

| | hundreds | tens | ones | |
|---|---|---|---|---|
| 3 hundreds + 4 tens + 8 ones = | 3 | 4 | 8 | = **348** |
| **2** hundreds + **1** ten + **7** ones = | 2 | 1 | 7 | = **217** |
| **6** hundreds + **3** tens + **5** ones = | 6 | 3 | 5 | = **635** |
| **4** hundreds + **7** tens + **9** ones = | 4 | 7 | 9 | = **479** |
| **2** hundreds + **9** tens + **4** ones = | 2 | 9 | 4 | = **294** |
| **4** hundreds + **2** tens + **0** ones = | 4 | 2 | 0 | = **420** |
| 3 hundreds + 1 ten + 3 ones = | **3** | **1** | **3** | = **313** |
| 3 hundreds + **5** tens + 7 ones = | **3** | 5 | **7** | = **348** |
| 6 hundreds + 2 tens + **8** ones = | **6** | 2 | 8 | = **628** |

Page 8

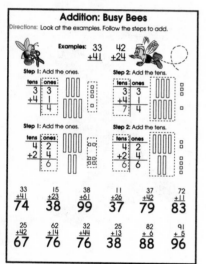

**Addition: Busy Bees**

Directions: Look at the examples. Follow the steps to add.

Examples: 33 +41    42 +24

Step 1: Add the ones.    Step 2: Add the tens.
Step 1: Add the ones.    Step 2: Add the tens.

| 33 +41 = **74** | 15 +23 = **38** | 38 +61 = **99** | 11 +26 = **37** | 37 +42 = **79** | 72 +11 = **83** |

| 25 +42 = **67** | 62 +14 = **76** | 32 +44 = **76** | 25 +13 = **38** | 82 +6 = **88** | 91 +5 = **96** |

Page 9

**Addition: Anchors Away**

Directions: Solve the addition problems. Use the code to find the answer to this riddle:

What did the pirate have to do before every trip out to sea?

| 48 | 36 | 58 | 96 | 69 | 75 | 89 | 29 |
|---|---|---|---|---|---|---|---|
| O | H | G | B | T | E | N | A |

42+16 = **58**  34+41 = **75**  60+9 = **69**     17+31 = **48**  55+34 = **89**
G   E   T              O   N

26+43 = **69**  14+22 = **36**  52+23 = **75**     83+13 = **96**  24+24 = **48**  5+24 = **29**  52+17 = **69**
T   H   E              B   O   A   T!

Page 10

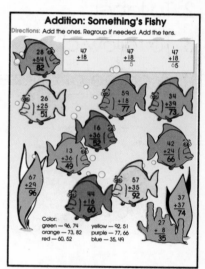

**Addition: Something's Fishy**

Directions: Add the ones. Regroup if needed. Add the tens.

47 +18 = 82    47 +18 = 5    47 +18 = 65

28 +54 = **82**    26 +25 = **51**    59 +18 = **77**    34 +39 = **73**

16 +36 = **52**    13 +36 = **49**    42 +24 = **66**

67 +29 = **96**    57 +35 = **92**    44 +16 = **60**    37 +37 = **74**

27 +8 = **35**

Color:
green — 96, 74     yellow — 92, 51
orange — 73, 82    purple — 77, 66
red — 60, 52       blue — 35, 49

Page 11

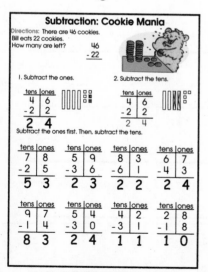

**Subtraction: Cookie Mania**

Directions: There are 46 cookies. Bill eats 22 cookies. How many are left?

46 - 22

1. Subtract the ones.    2. Subtract the tens.

| tens | ones | | tens | ones |
|---|---|---|---|---|
| 4 | 6 | | 4 | 6 |
| -2 | 2 | | -2 | 2 |
| 2 | 4 | | 2 | 4 |

Subtract the ones first. Then, subtract the tens.

| tens ones | tens ones | tens ones | tens ones |
|---|---|---|---|
| 7 8 -2 5 = **5 3** | 5 9 -3 6 = **2 3** | 8 3 -6 1 = **2 2** | 6 7 -4 3 = **2 4** |
| 9 7 -1 4 = **8 3** | 5 4 -3 0 = **2 4** | 4 2 -3 1 = **1 1** | 2 8 -1 8 = **1 0** |

Page 12

**Subtraction: Mountaintop Getaway**

Directions: Solve the problems. Find a path to the cabin by shading in all answers that have a 3 in them.

| 98 -52 = 46 | 46 -12 = 34 | 68 -17 = 51 |
| 79 -53 = 26 | 65 -23 = 42 | 63 -31 = 32 | 86 -32 = 54 |
| 59 -45 = 14 | 75 -64 = 11 | 67 -24 = 43 | 87 -54 = 33 | 55 -43 = 12 |
| 87 -65 = 22 | 44 -32 = 12 | 57 -24 = 33 | 88 -25 = 63 | 75 -61 = 14 | 48 -26 = 22 |
| 69 -25 = 44 | 95 -24 = 71 | 48 -13 = 35 | 58 -16 = 42 | 35 -13 = 22 | 39 -17 = 22 |

SECRET PATHS

Page 13

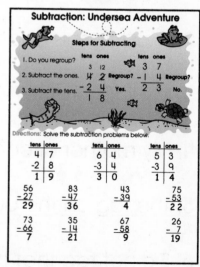

**Subtraction: Undersea Adventure**

Steps for Subtracting

| | tens ones | | tens ones |
|---|---|---|---|
| 1. Do you regroup? | 3 12 | | |
| 2. Subtract the ones. | 4 2  Regroup? | | 1 4  Regroup? |
| 3. Subtract the tens. | -2 4  Yes. | | 2 3  No. |
| | 1 8 | | |

Directions: Solve the subtraction problems below.

| tens ones | tens ones | tens ones |
|---|---|---|
| 4 7 -2 8 = **1 9** | 6 4 -3 4 = **3 0** | 5 3 -3 9 = **1 4** |

| 56 -27 = **29** | 83 -47 = **36** | 43 -39 = **4** | 75 -53 = **22** |

| 73 -66 = **7** | 35 -14 = **21** | 67 -58 = **9** | 26 -7 = **19** |

Page 14

Summer Link Basic Learning Skills Grade 3     84

## Page 15

### Addition and Subtraction: Go "Fore" It!

Directions: Add or subtract using regrouping.

| tens | ones |
|---|---|
| 2 | 15 |
| 3̶ | 5̶ |
| -2 | 7 |
|  | 8 |

$56 - 27 = 29$

$40 - 16 = 24$

$42 - 14 = 28$

$97 - 48 = 49$

$44 + 28 = 72$

$93 - 39 = 54$

$56 - 17 = 39$

$68 - 49 = 19$

$73 - 24 = 49$

$33 + 18 = 51$

$77 - 68 = 9$

$27 + 19 = 46$

$49 + 32 = 81$

## Page 16

### Place Value: Hundreds

The place value of a digit or numeral is shown by where it is in the number. For example, in the number 123, 1 has the place value of hundreds, 2 is tens, and 3 is ones.

Directions: Study the examples. Then write the missing numbers in the blanks.

Examples:

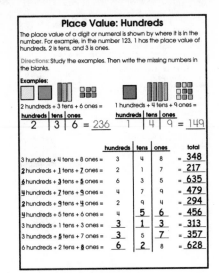

2 hundreds + 3 tens + 6 ones =

| hundreds | tens | ones |
|---|---|---|
| 2 | 3 | 6 | = 236 |

1 hundreds + 4 tens + 9 ones =

| hundreds | tens | ones |
|---|---|---|
| 1 | 4 | 9 | = 149 |

| | hundreds | tens | ones | total |
|---|---|---|---|---|
| 3 hundreds + 4 tens + 8 ones = | 3 | 4 | 8 | = 348 |
| 2 hundreds + 1 tens + 7 ones = | 2 | 1 | 7 | = 217 |
| 6 hundreds + 3 tens + 5 ones = | 6 | 3 | 5 | = 635 |
| 4 hundreds + 7 tens + 9 ones = | 4 | 7 | 9 | = 479 |
| 2 hundreds + 9 tens + 4 ones = | 2 | 9 | 4 | = 294 |
| 4 hundreds + 5 tens + 6 ones = | 4 | 5 | 6 | = 456 |
| 3 hundreds + 1 tens + 3 ones = | 3 | 1 | 3 | = 313 |
| 3 hundreds + 5 tens + 7 ones = | 3 | 5 | 7 | = 357 |
| 6 hundreds + 2 tens + 8 ones = | 6 | 2 | 8 | = 628 |

## Page 17

### Addition: 3-Digit Regrouping

Directions: Study the example. Follow the steps to add. Regroup when needed.

Step 1: Add the ones.
Step 2: Add the tens.
Step 3: Add the hundreds.

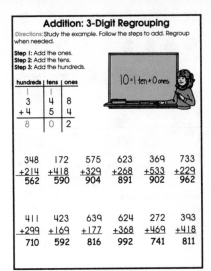

$10 = 1 \text{ ten} + 0 \text{ ones}$

| hundreds | tens | ones |
|---|---|---|
| 1 | | |
| 3 | 4 | 8 |
| + 4 | 5 | 4 |
| 8 | 0 | 2 |

$348 + 214 = 562$

$172 + 418 = 590$

$575 + 329 = 904$

$623 + 268 = 891$

$369 + 533 = 902$

$733 + 229 = 962$

$411 + 299 = 710$

$423 + 169 = 592$

$639 + 177 = 816$

$624 + 368 = 992$

$272 + 469 = 741$

$393 + 418 = 811$

## Page 18

### Addition: 3-Digit Regrouping

Directions: Study the example. Follow the steps to subtract.

Step 1: Regroup ones.
Step 2: Subtract ones.
Step 3: Subtract tens.
Step 4: Subtract hundreds.

Example:

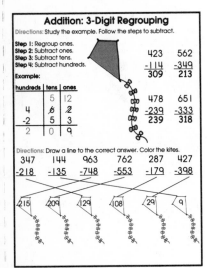

| hundreds | tens | ones |
|---|---|---|
| | 5 | 12 |
| 4 | 6̶ | 2̶ |
| -2 | 5 | 3 |
| 2 | 0 | 9 |

$423 - 114 = 309$

$562 - 349 = 213$

$478 - 239 = 239$

$651 - 333 = 318$

Directions: Draw a line to the correct answer. Color the kites.

$347 - 218$   $144 - 135$   $963 - 748$   $762 - 553$   $287 - 179$   $427 - 398$

215   209   129   108   29   9

## Page 20

### Graphs: Frog Bubbles

Directions: Complete the line graph to show how many bubbles each frog blew.

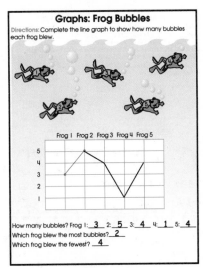

Frog 1  Frog 2  Frog 3  Frog 4  Frog 5

How many bubbles? Frog 1: **3**  2: **5**  3: **4**  4: **1**  5: **4**
Which frog blew the most bubbles? **2**
Which frog blew the fewest? **4**

## Page 21

### Numbers: Less Than, Greater Than

Directions: The open mouth points to the larger number. The small point goes to the smaller number. Draw the symbol < or > in the correct number.

Example:

5 ( > ) 3   This means that 5 is greater than 3, and 3 is less than 5.

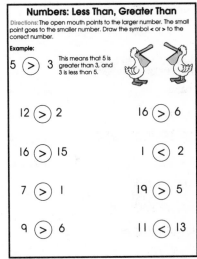

12 ( > ) 2        16 ( > ) 6

16 ( > ) 15       1 ( < ) 2

7 ( > ) 1         19 ( > ) 5

9 ( > ) 6         11 ( < ) 13

## Page 22

### Tables: Superstar Second Graders

Directions: Complete the table using the information shown. Then, answer the questions.

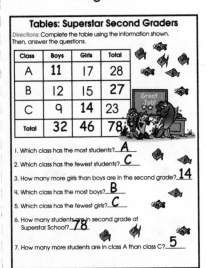

| Class | Boys | Girls | Total |
|---|---|---|---|
| A | 11 | 17 | 28 |
| B | 12 | 15 | 27 |
| C | 9 | 14 | 23 |
| Total | 32 | 46 | 78 |

1. Which class has the most students? **A**
2. Which class has the fewest students? **C**
3. How many more girls than boys are in the second grade? **14**
4. Which class has the most boys? **B**
5. Which class has the fewest girls? **C**
6. How many students are in second grade at Superstar School? **78**
7. How many more students are in class A than class C? **5**

## Page 23

### Fractions: Half, Third, Fourth

Directions: Color the correct fraction of each shape.

Examples:

shaded part 1 / equal parts 2 / $\frac{1}{2}$ (one-half)

shaded part 1 / equal parts 3 / $\frac{1}{3}$ (one-third)

shaded part 1 / equal parts 4 / $\frac{1}{4}$ (one-fourth)

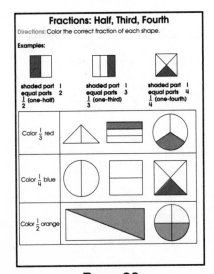

Color $\frac{1}{3}$ red

Color $\frac{1}{4}$ blue

Color $\frac{1}{2}$ orange

## Page 24

### Fractions: All Shapes and Sizes

Directions: Compare the fractions below. Write < or > in each box.

Examples:

$\frac{2}{4}$ < $\frac{3}{4}$   less than

$\frac{3}{4}$ > $\frac{2}{4}$   greater than

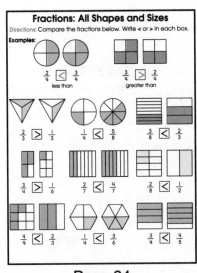

$\frac{2}{3}$ > $\frac{1}{3}$   $\frac{1}{4}$ < $\frac{5}{8}$   $\frac{3}{8}$ < $\frac{2}{3}$

$\frac{3}{4}$ > $\frac{1}{6}$   $\frac{2}{7}$ < $\frac{4}{7}$   $\frac{2}{8}$ < $\frac{1}{2}$

$\frac{4}{9}$ < $\frac{2}{3}$   $\frac{1}{4}$ < $\frac{3}{4}$   $\frac{3}{4}$ < $\frac{4}{5}$

## Fractions: Fun With Fractions

4 gloves are shaded. 9 gloves in all.

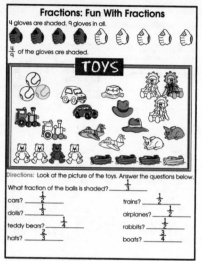

$\frac{4}{9}$ of the gloves are shaded.

**Directions:** Look at the picture of the toys. Answer the questions below.

What fraction of the balls is shaded? $\frac{1}{3}$

cars? $\frac{2}{4}$          trains? $\frac{1}{2}$

dolls? $\frac{1}{3}$          airplanes? $\frac{1}{2}$

teddy bears? $\frac{2}{4}$          rabbits? $\frac{1}{2}$

hats? $\frac{2}{3}$          boats? $\frac{3}{4}$

**Page 25**

---

## Fractions: Problem Solving

A fraction is a number that names part of a whole, such as $\frac{1}{2}$ or $\frac{1}{3}$.

**Directions:** Read each problem. Use the pictures to help you solve the problem. Write the fraction that answers the question.

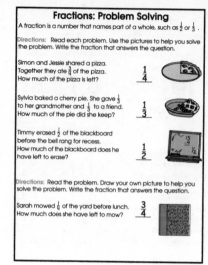

Simon and Jessie shared a pizza. Together they ate $\frac{3}{4}$ of the pizza. How much of the pizza is left? $\frac{1}{4}$

Sylvia baked a cherry pie. She gave $\frac{1}{3}$ to her grandmother and $\frac{1}{3}$ to a friend. How much of the pie did she keep? $\frac{1}{3}$

Timmy erased $\frac{1}{2}$ of the blackboard before the bell rang for recess. How much of the blackboard does he have left to erase? $\frac{1}{2}$

**Directions:** Read the problem. Draw your own picture to help you solve the problem. Write the fraction that answers the question.

Sarah mowed $\frac{1}{4}$ of the yard before lunch. How much does she have left to mow? $\frac{3}{4}$

**Page 26**

---

## Geometry

Geometry is mathematics that has to do with lines and shapes.

**Directions:** Color the shapes.

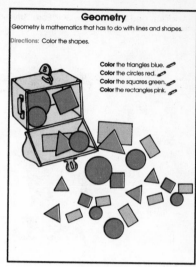

Color the triangles blue.
Color the circles red.
Color the squares green.
Color the rectangles pink.

**Page 27**

---

## Estimating: Inches

An inch is a unit of length in the standard measurement system.

**Directions:** Use a ruler to measure each object to the nearest inch.

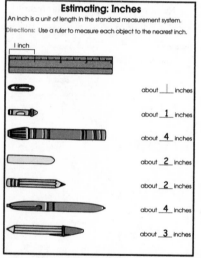

about __ inches

about 1 inches

about 4 inches

about 2 inches

about 2 inches

about 4 inches

about 3 inches

**Page 28**

---

## Telling Time: Hour, Half-Hour

An hour is sixty minutes. The short hand of a clock tells the hour. It is written **0:00**, such as **5:00**. A half-hour is thirty minutes. When the long hand of the clock is pointing to the six, the time is on the half-hour. It is written **:30**, such as **5:30**.

**Directions:** Study the examples. Tell what time it is on each clock.

**Examples:**

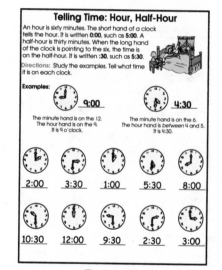

9:00
The minute hand is on the 12. The hour hand is on the 9. It is 9 o'clock.

4:30
The minute hand is on the 6. The hour hand is between 4 and 5. It is 4:30.

2:00     3:30     1:00     5:30     8:00

10:30     12:00     9:30     2:30     3:00

**Page 29**

---

## Telling Time: Quarter-Hours

Time can also be shown as fractions. 30 minutes = $\frac{1}{2}$ hour.

**Directions:** Shade the fraction of each clock and tell how many minutes you have shaded.

**Example:**

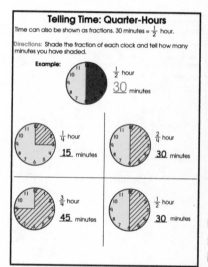

$\frac{1}{2}$ hour    30 minutes

$\frac{1}{4}$ hour    15 minutes

$\frac{2}{4}$ hour    30 minutes

$\frac{3}{4}$ hour    45 minutes

$\frac{1}{2}$ hour    30 minutes

**Page 30**

---

## Telling Time: Problem Solving

**Directions:** Solve each problem.

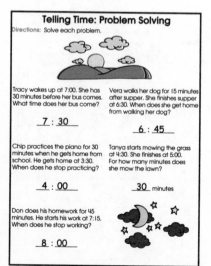

Tracy wakes up at 7:00. She has 30 minutes before her bus comes. What time does her bus come?

7 : 30

Vera walks her dog for 15 minutes after supper. She finishes supper at 6:30. When does she get home from walking her dog?

6 : 45

Chip practices the piano for 30 minutes when he gets home from school. He gets home at 3:30. When does he stop practicing?

4 : 00

Tanya starts mowing the grass at 4:30. She finishes at 5:00. For how many minutes does she mow the lawn?

30 minutes

Don does his homework for 45 minutes. He starts his work at 7:15. When does he stop working?

8 : 00

**Page 31**

---

## Telling Time: Time to Play Ball

**Directions:** Write the number of the matching clock in front of each sentence.

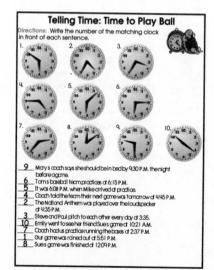

9  Mary's coach says she should be in bed by 9:30 P.M. the night before a game.

6  Tom's baseball team practices at 6:15 P.M.

5  It was 6:08 P.M. when Mike arrived at practice.

4  Coach told the team their next game was tomorrow at 4:45 P.M.

2  The National Anthem was played over the loudspeaker at 4:35 P.M.

3  Steve and Paul pitch to each other every day at 3:35.

10  Emily went to see her friend Sue's game at 10:21 A.M.

7  Coach had us practice running the bases at 2:37 P.M.

1  Our game was rained out at 5:51 P.M.

8  Sue's game was finished at 12:09 P.M.

**Page 32**

---

## Money: Penny, Nickel, Dime

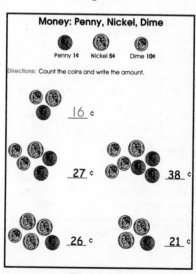

Penny 1¢     Nickel 5¢     Dime 10¢

**Directions:** Count the coins and write the amount.

16 ¢

27 ¢          38 ¢

26 ¢          21 ¢

**Page 33**

---

## Money: Quarter

A quarter is worth 25¢.

Directions: Count the coins and write the amounts.

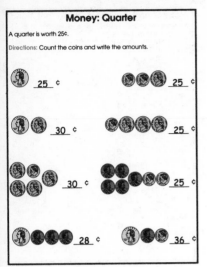

_25_ ¢     _25_ ¢

_30_ ¢     _25_ ¢

_30_ ¢     _25_ ¢

_28_ ¢     _36_ ¢

### Page 34

## Money: Problem Solving

Directions: Read each problem. Use the pictures to help you solve the problems.

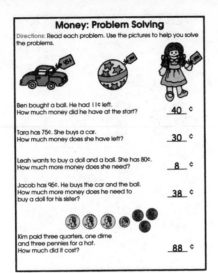

Ben bought a ball. He had 11¢ left.
How much money did he have at the start?    _40_ ¢

Tara has 75¢. She buys a car.
How much money does she have left?    _30_ ¢

Leah wants to buy a doll and a ball. She has 80¢.
How much more money does she need?    _8_ ¢

Jacob has 95¢. He buys the car and the ball.
How much more money does he need to
buy a doll for his sister?    _38_ ¢

Kim paid three quarters, one dime
and three pennies for a hat.
How much did it cost?    _88_ ¢

### Page 35

## Money: Dollar

One dollar equals 100 cents. It is written $1.00.

Directions: Count the money and write the amounts.

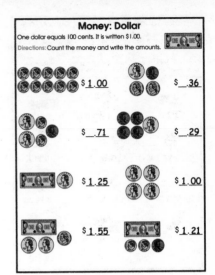

$ _1.00_     $ _.36_

$ _.71_     $ _.29_

$ _1.25_     $ _1.00_

$ _1.55_     $ _1.21_

### Page 36

## Money: Review

Directions: Add the money and write the total.

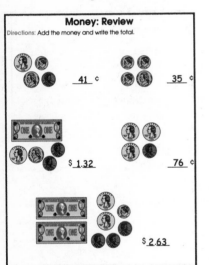

_41_ ¢     _35_ ¢

$ _1.32_     _76_ ¢

$ _2.63_

### Page 37

## Multiplication: Multiplying Creatures

Multiplication is a short way to find the sum of adding the same number a certain amount of times. For example, 7 x 4 = 28 instead of 7 + 7 + 7 + 7 = 28.

Directions: Study the example. Solve the problems.

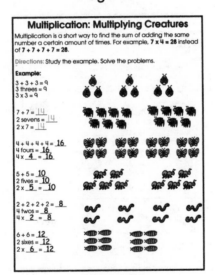

Example:
3 + 3 + 3 = 9
3 threes = 9
3 x 3 = 9

7 + 7 = _14_
2 sevens = _14_
2 x 7 = _14_

4 + 4 + 4 + 4 = _16_
4 fours = _16_
4 x _4_ = _16_

5 + 5 = _10_
2 fives = _10_
2 x _5_ = _10_

2 + 2 + 2 + 2 = _8_
4 twos = _8_
4 x _2_ = _8_

6 + 6 = _12_
2 sixes = _12_
2 x _6_ = _12_

### Page 38

## Multiplication: Drawing Groups

Multiplication is repeated addition.

Directions: Draw a picture for each problem. Then write the missing numbers.

Example:
Draw 2 groups of three apples.

3 + 3 = 6
or   2 x 3 = 6

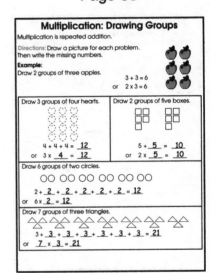

| Draw 3 groups of four hearts. | Draw 2 groups of five boxes. |
|---|---|
| 4 + 4 + 4 = _12_ | 5 + _5_ = _10_ |
| or   3 x _4_ = _12_ | or   2 x _5_ = _10_ |

Draw 6 groups of two circles.

2 + _2_ + _2_ + _2_ + _2_ + _2_ = _12_
or   6 x _2_ = _12_

Draw 7 groups of three triangles.

3 + _3_ + _3_ + _3_ + _3_ + _3_ + _3_ = _21_
or   _7_ x _3_ = _21_

### Page 39

## Multiplication: Review

Directions: Solve the problems.

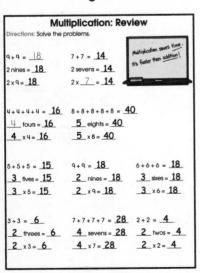

Multiplication saves time. It's faster than addition!

9 + 9 = _18_    7 + 7 = _14_
2 nines = _18_    2 sevens = _14_
2 x 9 = _18_    2 x _7_ = _14_

4 + 4 + 4 + 4 = _16_    8 + 8 + 8 + 8 + 8 = _40_
_4_ fours = _16_    _5_ eights = _40_
_4_ x 4 = _16_    _5_ x 8 = _40_

5 + 5 + 5 = _15_    9 + 9 = _18_    6 + 6 + 6 = _18_
_3_ fives = _15_    _2_ nines = _18_    _3_ sixes = _18_
_3_ x 5 = _15_    _2_ x 9 = _18_    _3_ x 6 = _18_

3 + 3 = _6_    7 + 7 + 7 + 7 = _28_    2 + 2 = _4_
_2_ threes = _6_    _4_ sevens = _28_    _2_ twos = _4_
_2_ x 3 = _6_    _4_ x 7 = _28_    _2_ x 2 = _4_

### Page 40

## Sound Spelling Review: Long and Short Vowels

Directions: Read the words in each box. Cross out the word that does not belong.

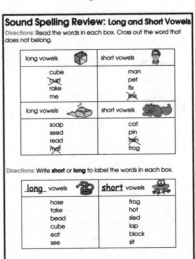

| long vowels | short vowels |
|---|---|
| cube | man |
| ~~cup~~ | pet |
| rake | fix |
| me | ~~ice~~ |

| long vowels | short vowels |
|---|---|
| soap | cat |
| seed | pin |
| read | ~~rain~~ |
| ~~mat~~ | frog |

Directions: Write **short** or **long** to label the words in each box.

| _long_ vowels | _short_ vowels |
|---|---|
| hose | frog |
| take | hot |
| bead | sled |
| cube | lap |
| eat | block |
| see | sit |

### Page 41

## Tricky Sound Spellings: R-Controlled Vowels

When a vowel is followed by the letter r, it has a different sound.

Example: **he** and **her**

Directions: Write a word from the word box to finish each sentence. Notice the sound of the vowel followed by an r.

| park | chair | horse | bark | bird |
|---|---|---|---|---|
| hurt | girl | hair | store | ears |

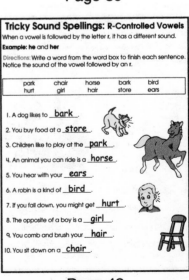

1. A dog likes to _bark_ .
2. You buy food at a _store_ .
3. Children like to play at the _park_ .
4. An animal you can ride is a _horse_ .
5. You hear with your _ears_ .
6. A robin is a kind of _bird_ .
7. If you fall down, you might get _hurt_ .
8. The opposite of a boy is a _girl_ .
9. You comb and brush your _hair_ .
10. You sit down on a _chair_ .

### Page 42

## Tricky Sound Spellings: ou, ow, au, aw

The vowel teams **ou** and **ow** can have the same sound. You can hear it in the words **clown** and **cloud**. The vowel teams **au** and **aw** have the same sound. You hear it in the words **because** and **law**.

**Directions:** Look at the pictures. Write the correct vowel team to complete the words. The first one is done for you. You may need to use a dictionary to help you with the correct spelling.

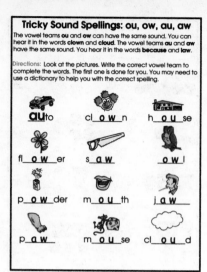

**au**to    cl**ow**n    h**ou**se

fl**ow**er    s**aw**    **ow**l

p**ow**der    m**ou**th    j**aw**

p**aw**    m**ou**se    cl**ou**d

**Page 43**

## Tricky Sound Spellings: oi, oy, ou, ow

**Directions:** Look at the first picture in each row. Circle the pictures that have the same sound.

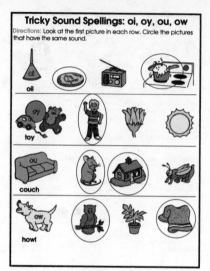

oil

toy

couch

howl

**Page 44**

## Tricky Sound Spellings: Consonant Blends

**Blends** are 2 or 3 consonant letters whose sounds combine, or blend, in a word, such as **tr** in **tree**.
**Directions:** Fill in the circle beside the missing blend in each word.

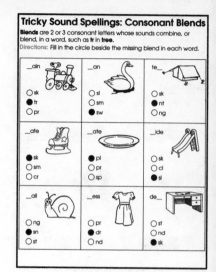

| _ain | _an | te_ |
|---|---|---|
| ○ sk | ○ sl | ○ sk |
| ● tr | ○ sm | ● nt |
| ○ pr | ● sw | ○ ng |
| _ate | _ate | _ide |
| ● sk | ● pl | ○ sk |
| ○ sm | ○ pr | ○ cl |
| ○ cr | ○ sp | ● sl |
| _ail | _ess | de_ |
| ○ ng | ○ pr | ○ st |
| ● sn | ● dr | ○ nd |
| ○ st | ○ nd | ● sk |

**Page 45**

## Tricky Sound Spellings: ch, sh, th, wh

**Directions:** Fill in the circle beside the missing sound in each word.

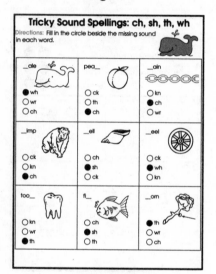

| _ale | pea_ | _ain |
|---|---|---|
| ● wh | ○ ck | ○ kn |
| ○ wr | ○ th | ● ch |
| ○ ch | ● ch | ○ wr |
| _imp | _ell | _eel |
| ○ ck | ○ ch | ○ ck |
| ○ kn | ● sh | ● wh |
| ● ch | ○ ck | ○ kn |
| too_ | fi_ | _orn |
| ○ kn | ○ ch | ● th |
| ○ wr | ● sh | ○ wr |
| ● th | ○ th | ○ ch |

**Page 46**

## Tricky Sound Spellings: Silent Letters

Some words have letters you can't hear at all, such as the **gh** in **night**, the **w** in **wrong**, the **l** in **walk**, the **k** in **knee**, the **b** in **climb**, and the **t** in **listen**.

**Directions:** Look at the words in the word box. Write the word under its picture. Underline the silent letters.

| knife | light | calf | wrench | lamb | eight |
| wrist | whistle | comb | thumb | knob | knee |

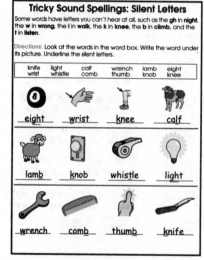

ei**gh**t    **w**rist    **k**nee    ca**l**f

lam**b**    **k**no**b**    **wh**is**t**le    li**gh**t

**w**rench    com**b**    t**h**um**b**    **k**nife

**Page 47**

## Contractions

**Directions:** Match the words with their contractions.

would not — wouldn't
was not — wasn't
he will — he'll
could not — couldn't
I have — I've

**Directions:** Make the words at the end of each line into contractions to complete the sentences.

1. He **didn't** know the answer.    **did not**
2. **It's** a long way home.    **It is**
3. **Here's** my house.    **Here is**
4. **We're** not going to school today.    **We are**
5. **They'll** take the bus home tomorrow.    **They will**

**Page 48**

## Compound Words

**Compound words** are formed by putting together two smaller words.

**Directions:** Help the cook brew her stew. Mix words from the first column with words from the second column to make new words. Write your new words on the lines at the bottom.

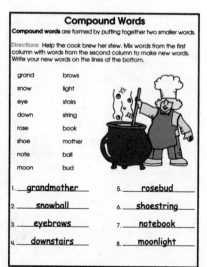

| grand | brows |
| snow | light |
| eye | stairs |
| down | string |
| rose | book |
| shoe | mother |
| note | ball |
| moon | bud |

1. grandmother    5. rosebud
2. snowball    6. shoestring
3. eyebrows    7. notebook
4. downstairs    8. moonlight

**Page 49**

## Compound Words

**Directions:** Draw a line under the compound word in each sentence. On the line, write the two words that make up the compound word.

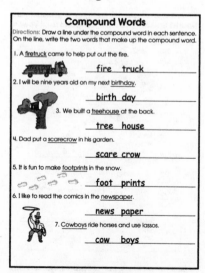

1. A firetruck came to help put out the fire.
   fire    truck
2. I will be nine years old on my next birthday.
   birth    day
3. We built a treehouse at the back.
   tree    house
4. Dad put a scarecrow in his garden.
   scare    crow
5. It is fun to make footprints in the snow.
   foot    prints
6. I like to read the comics in the newspaper.
   news    paper
7. Cowboys ride horses and use lassos.
   cow    boys

**Page 50**

## Synonyms

**Synonyms** are words that have almost the same meaning.

**Directions:** Read the story. Then fill in the blanks with the synonyms.

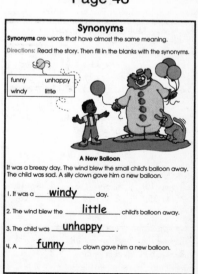

| funny | unhappy |
| windy | little |

**A New Balloon**

It was a breezy day. The wind blew the small child's balloon away. The child was sad. A silly clown gave him a new balloon.

1. It was a **windy** day.
2. The wind blew the **little** child's balloon away.
3. The child was **unhappy**.
4. A **funny** clown gave him a new balloon.

**Page 51**

## Antonyms

Antonyms are words that mean the opposite of another word.

**Examples:**
   **hot** and **cold**
   **short** and **tall**

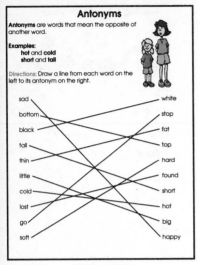

Directions: Draw a line from each word on the left to its antonym on the right.

| | |
|---|---|
| sad | white |
| bottom | stop |
| black | fat |
| tall | top |
| thin | hard |
| little | found |
| cold | short |
| lost | hot |
| go | big |
| soft | happy |

### Page 52

## Homophones

Homophones are words that sound the same but have different spellings and meanings, such as **see** and **sea**.

Directions: Match each word with its homophone.

| | |
|---|---|
| eight | blew |
| buy | whole |
| pail | ate |
| red | pale |
| hole | read |
| blue | hour |
| our | by |

Directions: Choose 3 homophone pairs and write sentences using them.

1. _____ Answers will vary. _____

2. _____

3. _____

### Page 53

## Syllables

Words are made up of parts called **syllables**. Each syllable has a vowel sound. One way to count syllables is to clap as you say the word.

**Example:**

| | | |
|---|---|---|
| cat | 1 clap | 1 syllable |
| table | 2 claps | 2 syllables |
| butterfly | 3 claps | 3 syllables |

Direction: "Clap out" the words below. Write how many syllables each word has.

| | | | |
|---|---|---|---|
| movie | 2 | dog | 1 |
| piano | 3 | basket | 2 |
| tree | 1 | swimmer | 2 |
| bicycle | 3 | rainbow | 2 |
| sun | 1 | paper | 2 |
| cabinet | 3 | picture | 2 |
| football | 2 | run | 1 |
| television | 4 | enter | 2 |

### Page 54

## Prefixes

Directions: Change the meaning of the sentences by adding the prefixes to the **bold** words.

The boy was **lucky** because he guessed the answer **correctly**.
The boy was (un) __unlucky__ because he guessed the answer (in) __incorrectly__ .

When Mary **behaved**, she felt **happy**.
When Mary (mis) __misbehaved__ ,
she felt (un) __unhappy__ .

Mike wore his jacket **buttoned** because the dance was **formal**.
Mike wore his jacket (un) __unbuttoned__ because the dance was (in) __informal__ .

Tim **understood** because he was **familiar** with the book.
Tim (mis) __misunderstood__ because he was (un) __unfamiliar__ with the book.

### Page 55

## Suffixes

Adding **ing** to the end of a word means that it is happening now. Adding **ed** to the end of a word means it happened in the past.

Directions: Look at the words in the word box. Underline the root word in each one. Write a word to complete each sentence.

| | | | | |
|---|---|---|---|---|
| snowing | wished | played | looking | crying |
| talking | walked | eating | going | doing |

1. We like to play. We __played__ yesterday.
2. Is that snow? Yes, it is __snowing__ .
3. Do you want to go with me? No, I am __going__ with my friend.
4. The baby will cry if we leave. The baby is __crying__ .
5. We will walk home from school. We __walked__ to school this morning.
6. Did you wish for a new bike? Yes, I __wished__ for one.
7. Who is going to do it while we are away? I am __doing__ it.
8. Did you talk to your friend? Yes, we are __talking__ now.
9. Will you look at my book? I am __looking__ at it now.
10. I like to eat pizza. We are __eating__ it today.

### Page 56

## Building a Sentence: Nouns

A **noun** is the name of a person, place, or thing.

Directions: Read the story and circle all the nouns. Then write the nouns next to the pictures below.

Our family likes to go to the park.
We play on the swings.
We eat cake.
We drink lemonade.
We throw the ball to our dog.
Then we go home.

| | |
|---|---|
| | family |
| | park |
| | swings |
| | cake |
| | lemonade |
| | ball |
| | dog |
| | home |

### Page 57

## Building a Sentence: Proper Nouns

**Proper nouns** are the names of specific people, places, and pets. **Proper nouns** begin with a capital letter.

Directions: Write capital letters where they should appear in the sentences below.

**Example:** joe can play in january.
      Joe can play in January.

1. we celebrate thanksgiving on the fourth thursday in november.

__We celebrate Thanksgiving on the third Thursday in November.__

2. in june, michelle and mark will go camping every friday.

__In June, Michelle and Mark will go camping every Friday.__

3. on mondays in october, i will take piano lessons.

__On Mondays in October, I will take piano lessons.__

### Page 58

## Building a Sentence: Adjectives

**Adjectives** are words that tell more about a person, place, or thing.

**Examples:** cold, fuzzy, dark

Directions: Think of your own adjectives. Write a story about Fluffy the cat.

Answers will vary.

1. Fluffy is a _____ cat.
2. The color of his fur is _____ .
3. He likes to chew on my _____ shoes.
4. He likes to eat _____ cat food.
5. I like Fluffy because he is so _____ .

### Page 59

## Building a Sentence: Pronouns

**Pronouns** are words that can be used instead of nouns. **She**, **he**, **it**, and **they** are pronouns.

Directions: Read the sentence. Then write the sentence again, using **she**, **he**, **it**, or **they** in the blank.

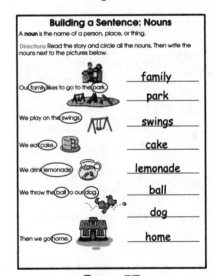

1. Dan likes funny jokes. __He__ likes funny jokes.
2. Peg and Sam went to the zoo. __They__ went to the zoo.
3. My dog likes to dig in the yard. __It__ likes to dig in the yard.
4. Sara is a very good dancer. __She__ is a very good dancer.
5. Fred and Ted are twins. __They__ are twins.

### Page 60

## Building a Sentence: Ownership

We add **'s** to nouns (people, places, or things) to tell who or what owns something.

**Directions:** Read the sentences. Fill in the blanks to show ownership.

**Example:** The doll belongs to **Sara**.
It is **Sara's** doll.

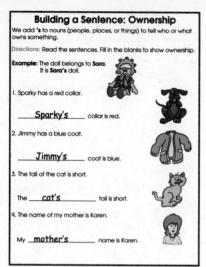

1. Sparky has a red collar.

_____**Sparky's**_____ collar is red.

2. Jimmy has a blue coat.

_____**Jimmy's**_____ coat is blue.

3. The tail of the cat is short.

The _____**cat's**_____ tail is short.

4. The name of my mother is Karen.

My _____**mother's**_____ name is Karen.

### Page 61

## Building a Sentence: Verbs

We use **verbs** to tell when something happens. Sometimes we add an **ed** to verbs that tell us if something has already happened.

**Example:** Today, we will **play**. Yesterday, we **played**.

**Directions:** Write the correct verb in the blank.

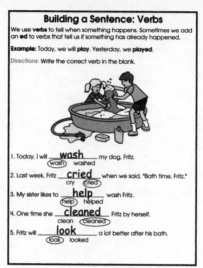

1. Today, I will **wash** my dog, Fritz.
(wash) washed

2. Last week, Fritz **cried** when we said, "Bath time, Fritz."
cry (cried)

3. My sister likes to **help** wash Fritz.
(help) helped

4. One time she **cleaned** Fritz by herself.
clean (cleaned)

5. Fritz will **look** a lot better after his bath.
(look) looked

### Page 62

## Building a Sentence: Verbs

**Directions:** Write each verb in the correct column.

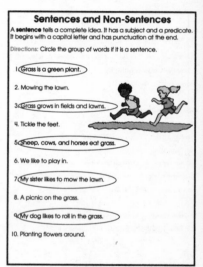

| rake | talked | look | hopped | skip |
| cooked | fished | call | clean | sewed |

| Yesterday | Today |
|---|---|
| cooked | rake |
| talked | look |
| fished | call |
| hopped | clean |
| sewed | skip |

### Page 63

## Building a Sentence: Location Words

**Directions:** Use a location word to tell where the cat is in each sentence.

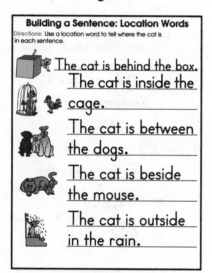

The cat is behind the box.
The cat is inside the cage.
The cat is between the dogs.
The cat is beside the mouse.
The cat is outside in the rain.

### Page 64

## Building a Sentence: Subject and Predicate

The **subject** part of the sentence is the person, place, or thing the sentence is about. The **predicate** is the part of the sentence that tells what the subject does.

**Directions:** Draw a line between the subject and the predicate. Underline the noun in the subject and circle the verb.

**Example:** The furry cat (ate) food.

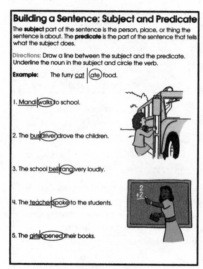

1. Mandi (walks) to school.

2. The bus driver (drove) the children.

3. The school bell (rang) very loudly.

4. The teacher (spoke) to the students.

5. The girls (opened) their books.

### Page 65

## Sentences and Non-Sentences

A **sentence** tells a complete idea. It has a subject and a predicate. It begins with a capital letter and has punctuation at the end.

**Directions:** Circle the group of words if it is a sentence.

1. (Grass is a green plant.)
2. Mowing the lawn.
3. (Grass grows in fields and lawns.)
4. Tickle the feet.
5. (Sheep, cows, and horses eat grass.)
6. We like to play in.
7. (My sister likes to mow the lawn.)
8. A picnic on the grass.
9. (My dog likes to roll in the grass.)
10. Planting flowers around.

### Page 66

## Reading for Sequence

**Directions:** Read about making clay. Then follow the instructions.

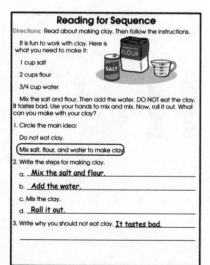

It is fun to work with clay. Here is what you need to make it:

1 cup salt
2 cups flour
3/4 cup water

Mix the salt and flour. Then add the water. DO NOT eat the clay. It tastes bad. Use your hands to mix and mix. Now, roll it out. What can you make with your clay?

1. Circle the main idea:
Do not eat clay.
(Mix salt, flour, and water to make clay)

2. Write the steps for making clay.
a. _Mix the salt and flour._
b. _Add the water._
c. Mix the clay.
d. _Roll it out._

3. Write why you should not eat clay. _It tastes bad._

### Page 67

## Reading for Sequence

Mrs. Posey made a new hat, but she forgot how she did it. When she tried to tell her friend, she got all mixed up.

**Directions:** Read Mrs. Posey's story. Write her story on the lines in the order you think it happened. Then color the picture.

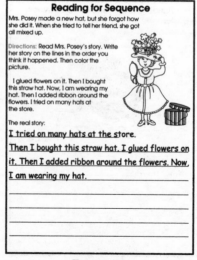

I glued flowers on it. Then I bought this straw hat. Now, I am wearing my hat. Then I added ribbon around the flowers. I tried on many hats at the store.

The real story:
I tried on many hats at the store.
Then I bought this straw hat. I glued flowers on it. Then I added ribbon around the flowers. Now, I am wearing my hat.

### Page 68

## Reading for Context Clues

**Directions:** Read the story. Use context clues to figure out the missing words. Write the words from the word box. Then, answer the questions.

| socks | scarf | sweaters | mittens |

Maria bundles up. She sticks her arms through two **sweaters**. She tugs three pairs of **socks** over her feet. She wraps a **scarf** around her neck. At last, she pulls her **mittens** onto her hands. Maria goes outside to play. Nobody is warmer than Maria.

1. What clue words helped you figure out sweaters?
**sticks her arms through**

2. What clue words helped you figure out mittens?
**onto her hands**

### Page 69

### Reading for Context Clues

Directions: Read the clues carefully. Then, number the cats. When you are sure you are correct, color the cats.

1. A gray cat sits on the gate.
2. A cat with orange and black spots sits near the tree.
3. A brown cat sits near the bush.
4. A white cat sits between the orange and black spotted cat and the gray cat.
5. A black cat sits next to the brown cat.
6. An orange cat sits between the gray cat and the black cat.

Page 70

### Reading for Plot and Setting

Stories have a setting and a plot. The **setting** tells where and when the story takes place. The **plot** tells what happened.

Directions: Read the story. Then, follow the directions below.

 Michael, Sam, and Dominic were best friends. They ate lunch together. At recess, they swung on the swings together. On the swings, Michael said, "Come to my house to play after school." Dominic thought Michael was looking at Sam. He waited for Michael to ask him, too, but Michael didn't. All afternoon, Dominic felt sad. When the bell rang, he started to go home. "Where are you going?" Michael called. "I wanted you both to come to my house." With a big smile, Dominic ran to join Michael and Sam.

Fill in the circle beside the words that tell about the story's setting.
- ○ After school at Sam's house
- ● At school on a school day
- ○ At the park on a Saturday

Number the plot events to show the order in which they happened.
- 2 Dominic felt sad because he thought he wasn't invited.
- 3 Dominic and Sam went to Michael's house.
- 1 Michael invited the boys over.

Page 71

### Reading for Details

Directions: Read the story. Then answer the questions.

Sometimes Marvin and Mugsy scratch and itch. Marcy knows that fleas or ticks are insect pests to her pets. Their bites are painful. Fleas suck the blood of animals. They don't have wings, but they can jump. Ticks are very flat, suck blood, and are related to spiders. They like to hide in dogs' ears. That is why Marcy checks Marvin and Mugsy every week for fleas and ticks.

1. What is a pest? __an insect such as a flea or tick__

2. List three facts about fleas.
   1) __They suck the blood of animals.__
   2) __They don't have wings.__
   3) __They can jump.__

3. List three facts about ticks.
   1) __They are very flat.__
   2) __They suck blood.__
   3) __They are related to spiders.__

Page 72

### Reading for Main Ideas

Directions: Read the story. Then answer the questions.

Tonda has many books. She gets different ideas from these books. Some of her books are about fish. Some are about cardboard and paper crafts. Some are about nature. Others are about reusing junk. Tonda wants to make a paper airplane. She reads about it in one of her books. Then she asks an adult to help her.

1. Circle the main idea:
   (Tonda learns about different ideas from books.)
   Tonda likes crafts.

2. (Circle the correct answer.) Tonda is:
   (a person who likes to read.)
   a person who doesn't like books.

3. What does Tonda want to make from paper? _____
   __an airplane__

4. Write two ways to learn how to do something.
   1) __Answers will vary.__
   2) _____

Page 73

### Reading for Main Ideas

Directions: Read the story. Then follow the instructions.

Angela learned a lot about sharks when her class visited the city aquarium. She learned that sharks are fish. Some sharks are as big as an elephant, and some can fit into a small paper bag. Sharks have no bones. They have hundreds of teeth, and when they lose them, they grow new ones. They eat animals of any kind. Whale sharks are the largest of all fish.

1. Circle the main idea:
   (Angela learned a lot about sharks at the aquarium.)
   Some sharks are as big as elephants.

2. When sharks lose teeth, they __grow new ones__
   _____

3. __Whale sharks__ are the largest of all fish.

4. Sharks have bones. (Circle the answer.)
   Yes    (No)

Page 74

### Reading for Main Ideas

Samantha thought of a good joke. She bragged that she could read Maria's mind. She put her hand on Maria's head, closed her eyes, and said, "You had red punch with your lunch!"
"Wow! You're right!" replied Maria, not realizing that she had a little red ring around her lips.
"That was easy. But I bet you can't tell me what I just ate," said Thomas.
"That's a bunch of baloney," answered Samantha.
"How did you know?" gasped Thomas.
"It's my little secret," said Samantha, with a sigh of relief.
"Here comes your mom," said Maria. "Can you read her mind, too?"
Samantha looked down at her watch. She should have been home half an hour ago. As she ran to meet her mother, she yelled back, "Yes, I know exactly what she's thinking!"

Directions: Make inferences about Samantha's mind-reading tricks. Fill in the circle beside the correct inference.

1. Was Samantha sure that Thomas had eaten bologna for lunch?
   - ● No, she was just lucky.
   - ○ Yes, she saw him eat his bologna sandwich.

2. What was Samantha's mother probably thinking?
   - ○ Samantha was a great mind reader.
   - ● Samantha was late.

Page 75

### Reading for Cause and Effect

Things that happen can make other things happen. The event that happens is the **effect**. Why the event happens is the **cause**.

**Example:** Marcie tripped on the step and fell down.
   **Cause:** Marcie tripped on the step.
   **Effect:** Marcie fell down.

Directions: Read the story.

Marcie knows a magic trick. She can make a ring seem to go up and down by itself on a pencil. Marcie has to get ready ahead of time. She ties a piece of skinny thread under the pencil's eraser. Then, she ties the thread to a button on her blouse. In front of her audience, Marcie puts a ring on the pencil. When Marcie leans forward, the thread goes loose, so the ring goes down. Then, Marcie leans back. The thread tightens and makes the ring go up the pencil.

Directions: Write the cause to complete each sentence.

1. The audience cannot see the thread because

   it is skinny.

2. Leaning forward

   makes the ring go down.

Page 76

### Reading: Predict What Happens

Directions: Read the story. Then answer the questions.

Marcy had a great idea for a game to play with her dogs, Marvin and Mugsy. The game was called "Dog Derby." Marcy would stand at one end of the driveway and hold on to the dogs by their collars. Her friend Mitch would stand at the other end of the driveway. When he said, "Go!" Marcy would let go of the dogs and they would race to Mitch. The first one there would get a dog biscuit. If there was a tie, both dogs would get a biscuit.

1. Who do you think will win the race?

Why?

2. What _____ happen when they race again?
   _____

Page 77

### Fiction: Made-Up Stories

Directions: **Fiction** is a make-believe story. Read the stories. Underline the sentence that makes each story fiction.

 Michelle got a kitten for her birthday. It was soft and cuddly. It liked to chase fuzzy toys. After playing, it napped in Michelle's lap. One day the kitten said to Michelle, "Would you like me to tell you a story?"

 The team lined up. The kicker kicked the football. Up, up it soared. It went up so high that it went into orbit around the Earth. The game was over. The Aardvarks had won.

 "This is a great car," the salesperson said. "It can go very fast. It can cook your breakfast. It always starts, even on the coldest day. You really should buy this car."

 Chris studied about healthy food in school. He learned that milk could make him grow. Chris drank a glass of milk just before he went to bed. When he got up in the morning, he was so tall, his head went right through the ceiling.

Page 78

## Nonfiction: True Facts

**Directions:** **Nonfiction** is a true story. Read about tornadoes. Then follow the instructions.

A tornado begins over land with strong winds and thunderstorms. The spinning air becomes a funnel. It can cause damage. If you are inside, go to the lowest floor of the building. A basement is a safe place. A bathroom or closet in the middle of a building can be a safe place, too. If you are outside, lie in a ditch. Remember, tornadoes are dangerous.

Write five facts about tornadoes.

**Answers may include:**

1. A tornado begins over land.

2. Spinning air becomes a funnel.

3. Tornadoes can cause damage.

4. A basement is a safe place to be in a tornado.

5. If you are outside during a tornado, you should lie in a ditch.

**Page 79**

---

## Fiction or Nonfiction: Which Is It?

**Directions:** Read about fiction and nonfiction books. Then follow the instructions.

There are many kinds of books. Some books have make-believe stories about princesses and dragons. Some books contain poetry and rhymes, like Mother Goose. These are fiction.

Some books contain facts about space and plants. And still other books have stories about famous people in history like Abraham Lincoln. These are nonfiction.

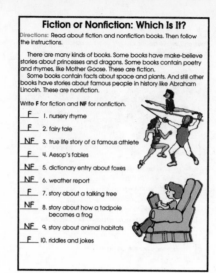

Write **F** for fiction and **NF** for nonfiction.

F  1. nursery rhyme

F  2. fairy tale

NF  3. true life story of a famous athlete

F  4. Aesop's fables

NF  5. dictionary entry about foxes

NF  6. weather report

F  7. story about a talking tree

NF  8. story about how a tadpole becomes a frog

NF  9. story about animal habitats

F  10. riddles and jokes

**Page 80**

---

## Learning Dictionary Skills: ABC Order

If the first letters of two words are the same, look at the second letters in both words. If the second letters are the same, look at the third letters.

**Directions:** Write 1, 2, 3, or 4 on the lines in each row to put the words in ABC order.

**Example:**

1. **1** candy  **2** carrot  **4** duck  **3** dance

2. **2** cold  **4** hot  **1** carry  **3** hit

3. **2** flash  **1** fan  **3** fun  **4** garden

4. **2** seat  **4** sun  **1** saw  **3** sit

5. **3** row  **1** ring  **2** rock  **4** run

6. **2** truck  **3** turn  **4** twin  **1** talk

7. **1** seven  **2** shoe  **4** soup  **3** smell

**Page 81**

---

## Learning Dictionary Skills

**Directions:** Look at this page from a picture dictionary. Then answer the questions.

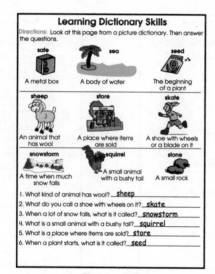

**safe** — A metal box
**sea** — A body of water
**seed** — The beginning of a plant
**sheep** — An animal that has wool
**store** — A place where items are sold
**skate** — A shoe with wheels or a blade on it
**snowstorm** — A time when much snow falls
**squirrel** — A small animal with a bushy tail
**stone** — A small rock

1. What kind of animal has wool? **sheep**
2. What do you call a shoe with wheels on it? **skate**
3. When a lot of snow falls, what is it called? **snowstorm**
4. What is a small animal with a bushy tail? **squirrel**
5. What is a place where items are sold? **store**
6. When a plant starts, what is it called? **seed**

**Page 82**

---

## Learning Dictionary Skills

When words have more than one meaning, the meanings are numbered in a dictionary.

**Directions:** Read the meanings of **tag**. Write the number of the correct definition after each sentence.

**tag**
1. A small strip or tab attached to something else
2. To label
3. To follow closely and constantly
4. A game of chase

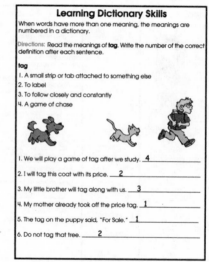

1. We will play a game of tag after we study. **4**

2. I will tag this coat with its price. **2**

3. My little brother will tag along with us. **3**

4. My mother already took off the price tag. **1**

5. The tag on the puppy said, "For Sale." **1**

6. Do not tag that tree. **2**

**Page 83**

---

# Developmental Skills for Third Grade Success

McGraw-Hill, the premier educational publisher PreK–12, wants to be your partner in helping you educate your child. *Summer Link Basic Learning Skills* was designed to help your child retain those skills learned during the past school year. With *Summer Link Basic Learning Skills*, your child will be ready to review and take on new material with confidence when he or she returns to school in the fall. The skills reviewed here will help your child be prepared for proficiency testing.

You can use this checklist to evaluate your child's progress. Place a check mark in the box if the appropriate skill has been mastered. If your child needs more work with a particular skill, place an "R" in the box and come back to it for review.

## Math Skills

☐ Counts by 2's to 100

☐ Counts by 5's to 100

☐ Counts by 10's to 100

☐ Recognizes number symbols 0—1,000

☐ Completes simple patterns

☐ Names basic geometric shapes

☐ Sort objects using at least one attribute

☐ Can add up to 100

☐ Can subtract from 100

☐ Interprets and creates graphs

☐ Indicates order using ordinal numbers

☐ Can identify > and < signs

☐ Can write fractions from numeric pictures

☐ Understands numbers having place values to 3 digits

☐ Completes two-digit addition; no regrouping

☐ Completes two-digit addition with regrouping

☐ Completes two-digit subtraction; no regrouping

☐ Completes two-digit subtraction with regrouping

☐ Completes three-digit addition; no regrouping

☐ Completes three-digit subtraction; no regrouping

☐ Performs (3 single digits) column addition

☐ Knows values of coins in combination

☐ Can solve money addition problems

☐ Can measure items using simple standard units

☐ Understands basic concept of multiplication

☐ Can tell time at various intervals

☐ Makes estimations based on past experiences

☐ Can name fractions of objects using 1/4, 1/3, and 1/2

☐ Uses problem-solving strategies

## Language Arts Skills

☐ Recognizes uppercase letters

☐ Recognizes lowercase letters

☐ Knows difference between consonants and vowels

☐ Knows the single letter sounds

☐ Knows digraphs ch, sh, th, wh

☐ Knows consonant and vowel blends

# Developmental Skills for Third Grade Success

## Language Arts Skills, continued

☐ Knows beginning, ending, and middle sounds of words

☐ Recognizes compound words

☐ Discriminates between antonyms and synonyms

☐ Discriminates between homophones and other words

Recognizes parts of speech:

    ☐ nouns and proper nouns

    ☐ verbs

    ☐ adjectives

    ☐ pronouns

    ☐ articles

☐ Knows how to create contractions

☐ Recognizes controlled vowels: er, ar, ir, ur, or

☐ Can break words into syllables

☐ Can look up words in a dictionary

☐ Correctly writes upper- and lowercase letters

Uses writing strategies:

    ☐ Uses knowledge of letter sounds to create words

    ☐ Copies or traces words

    ☐ Writing shows a sequence of events or clear ideas

    ☐ Ability to use rhymes

☐ Identifies types of sentences

☐ Can identify prefixes and suffixes

☐ Recognizes meaning and use of possessives

☐ Recognizes various tenses of verbs

☐ Identifies types of sentences

☐ Recognizes subject/predicate of a sentence

☐ Recognizes complete and incomplete sentences

☐ Uses correction punctuation: ., ?, !

☐ Recognizes misspelled words

## Reading Skills

Uses reading strategies.

    ☐ Uses pictures to tell a story

    ☐ Follows text from left to right

    ☐ Uses story content and pattern to predict

    ☐ Uses grammar to help decipher words

    ☐ Sounds out words

☐ Can interpret characters in a story

☐ Recalls main events in a story

☐ Recalls conflict of a story

☐ Recalls setting of a story

☐ Recalls conclusion of a story

☐ Recalls or predicts a simple sequence of events

☐ Recognizes causes and effects of situations

☐ Recognizes forms of literature (poetry, nonfiction, etc.)

# SPECTRUM

## PRESCHOOL

Learning Letters offers comprehensive instruction and practice in following directions, recognizing and writing upper- and lowercase letters, and beginning phonics. Math Readiness features activities that teach such important skills as counting, identifying numbers, creating patterns, and recognizing "same and different." Basic Concepts and Skills offers exercises that help preschoolers identify colors, read and write words, identify simple shapes, and more. 160 pages.

| TITLE | ISBN | PRICE |
|---|---|---|
| Learning Letters | 1-57768-329-3 | $8.95 |
| Math Readiness | 1-57768-339-0 | $8.95 |
| Basic Concepts and Skills | 1-57768-349-8 | $8.95 |

## DOLCH SIGHT WORD ACTIVITIES

The Dolch Sight Word Activities workbooks use the classic Dolch list of 220 basic vocabulary words that make up from 50 to 75 percent of all reading matter that children ordinarily encounter. Since these words are ordinarily recognized on sight, they are called sight words. Volume 1 includes 110 sight words. Volume 2 covers the remainder of the list. 160 pages. Answer key included.

| TITLE | ISBN | PRICE |
|---|---|---|
| Grades K-1 Vol. 1 | 1-56189-917-8 | $9.95 |
| Grades K-1 Vol. 2 | 1-56189-918-6 | $9.95 |

## ENRICHMENT MATH AND READING

Books in this series offer advanced math and reading for students excelling in grades 3–6. Lessons follow the same curriculum children are being taught in school while presenting the material in a way that children feel challenged. 160 pages. Answer key included.

| TITLE | ISBN | PRICE |
|---|---|---|
| Grade 3 | 1-57768-503-2 | $8.95 |
| Grade 4 | 1-57768-504-0 | $8.95 |
| Grade 5 | 1-57768-505-9 | $8.95 |
| Grade 6 | 1-57768-506-7 | $8.95 |

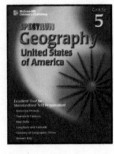

## GEOGRAPHY

Full-color, three-part lessons strengthen geography knowledge and map-reading skills. Focusing on five geographic themes including location, place, human/environmental interaction, movement, and regions. Over 150 pages. Glossary of geographical terms and answer key included.

| TITLE | ISBN | PRICE |
|---|---|---|
| Grade 3, Communities | 1-56189-963-1 | $8.95 |
| Grade 4, Regions | 1-56189-964-X | $8.95 |
| Grade 5, USA | 1-56189-965-8 | $8.95 |
| Grade 6, World | 1-56189-966-6 | $8.95 |

## LANGUAGE ARTS

Encourages creativity and builds confidence by making writing fun! Seventy-two four-part lessons strengthen writing skills by focusing on parts of speech, word usage, sentence structure, punctuation, and proofreading. Each book includes a Writer's Handbook at the end of the book that offers writing tips. This series is based on the highly respected SRA/McGraw-Hill language arts series. More than 180 full-color pages. Answer key included.

| TITLE | ISBN | PRICE |
|---|---|---|
| Grade 2 | 1-56189-952-6 | $8.95 |
| Grade 3 | 1-56189-953-4 | $8.95 |
| Grade 4 | 1-56189-954-2 | $8.95 |
| Grade 5 | 1-56189-955-0 | $8.95 |
| Grade 6 | 1-56189-956-9 | $8.95 |

## MATH

Features easy-to-follow instructions that give students a clear path to success. This series has comprehensive coverage of the basic skills, helping children to master math fundamentals. Over 150 pages. Answer key included.

| TITLE | ISBN | PRICE |
|---|---|---|
| Grade K | 1-56189-900-3 | $8.95 |
| Grade 1 | 1-56189-901-1 | $8.95 |
| Grade 2 | 1-56189-902-X | $8.95 |
| Grade 3 | 1-56189-903-8 | $8.95 |
| Grade 4 | 1-56189-904-6 | $8.95 |
| Grade 5 | 1-56189-905-4 | $8.95 |
| Grade 6 | 1-56189-906-2 | $8.95 |
| Grade 7 | 1-56189-907-0 | $8.95 |
| Grade 8 | 1-56189-908-9 | $8.95 |

## PHONICS/WORD STUDY

Provides everything children need to build multiple skills in language. Focusing on phonics, structural analysis, and dictionary skills, this series also offers creative ideas for using phonics and word study skills in other language areas. Over 200 pages. Answer key included.

| TITLE | ISBN | PRICE |
|---|---|---|
| Grade K | 1-56189-940-2 | $8.95 |
| Grade 1 | 1-56189-941-0 | $8.95 |
| Grade 2 | 1-56189-942-9 | $8.95 |
| Grade 3 | 1-56189-943-7 | $8.95 |
| Grade 4 | 1-56189-944-5 | $8.95 |
| Grade 5 | 1-56189-945-3 | $8.95 |
| Grade 6 | 1-56189-946-1 | $8.95 |

## READING

This full-color series creates an enjoyable reading environment, even for below-average readers. Each book contains captivating content, colorful characters, and compelling illustrations, so children are eager to find out what happens next. Over 150 pages. Answer key included.

| TITLE | ISBN | PRICE |
|---|---|---|
| Grade K | 1-56189-910-0 | $8.95 |
| Grade 1 | 1-56189-911-9 | $8.95 |
| Grade 2 | 1-56189-912-7 | $8.95 |
| Grade 3 | 1-56189-913-5 | $8.95 |
| Grade 4 | 1-56189-914-3 | $8.95 |
| Grade 5 | 1-56189-915-1 | $8.95 |
| Grade 6 | 1-56189-916-X | $8.95 |

## SPELLING

This full-color series links spelling to reading and writing, and increases skills in words and meanings, consonant and vowel spellings, and proofreading practice. Over 200 pages. Speller dictionary and answer key included.

| TITLE | ISBN | PRICE |
|---|---|---|
| Grade 1 | 1-56189-921-6 | $8.95 |
| Grade 2 | 1-56189-922-4 | $8.95 |
| Grade 3 | 1-56189-923-2 | $8.95 |
| Grade 4 | 1-56189-924-0 | $8.95 |
| Grade 5 | 1-56189-925-9 | $8.95 |
| Grade 6 | 1-56189-926-7 | $8.95 |

## VOCABULARY

An essential building block for writing and reading proficiency, this series extends vocabulary knowledge through key concepts based on language arts and reading standards, offering a solid foundation for language arts, spelling, and reading comprehension. The series features a proficiency test practice section for standards-aligned assessment. Over 150 pages. Answer key included.

| TITLE | ISBN | PRICE |
|---|---|---|
| Grade 3 | 1-57768-903-8 | $8.95 |
| Grade 4 | 1-57768-904-6 | $8.95 |
| Grade 5 | 1-57768-905-4 | $8.95 |
| Grade 6 | 1-57768-906-2 | $8.95 |

## WRITING

Lessons focus on creative and expository writing using clearly stated objectives and pre-writing exercises. Eight essential reading skills are applied. Activities include main idea, sequence, comparison, detail, fact and opinion, cause and effect, making a point, and point of view. Over 130 pages. Answer key included.

| TITLE | ISBN | PRICE |
|---|---|---|
| Grade 1 | 1-56189-931-3 | $8.95 |
| Grade 2 | 1-56189-932-1 | $8.95 |
| Grade 3 | 1-56189-933-X | $8.95 |
| Grade 4 | 1-56189-934-8 | $8.95 |
| Grade 5 | 1-56189-935-6 | $8.95 |
| Grade 6 | 1-56189-936-4 | $8.95 |
| Grade 7 | 1-56189-937-2 | $8.95 |
| Grade 8 | 1-56189-938-0 | $8.95 |

## TEST PREP

Prepares children to do their best on current editions of the five major standardized tests. Activities reinforce test-taking skills through examples, tips, practice, and timed exercises. Subjects include reading, math, language arts, writing, social studies, and science. Over 150 pages. Answer key included.

| TITLE | ISBN | PRICE |
|---|---|---|
| Grades 1-2 | 1-57768-672-1 | $9.95 |
| Grade 3 | 1-57768-673-X | $9.95 |
| Grade 4 | 1-57768-674-8 | $9.95 |
| Grade 5 | 1-57768-675-6 | $9.95 |
| Grade 6 | 1-57768-676-4 | $9.95 |
| Grade 7 | 1-57768-677-2 | $9.95 |
| Grade 8 | 1-57768-678-0 | $9.95 |

All our workbooks meet school curriculum guidelines and correspond to
The McGraw-Hill Companies' classroom textbooks. Prices subject to change without notice.